1,000,000 Books

are available to read at

Forgotten Books

www.ForgottenBooks.com

Read online
Download PDF
Purchase in print

ISBN 978-1-333-57632-5
PIBN 10521842

This book is a reproduction of an important historical work. Forgotten Books uses state-of-the-art technology to digitally reconstruct the work, preserving the original format whilst repairing imperfections present in the aged copy. In rare cases, an imperfection in the original, such as a blemish or missing page, may be replicated in our edition. We do, however, repair the vast majority of imperfections successfully; any imperfections that remain are intentionally left to preserve the state of such historical works.

Forgotten Books is a registered trademark of FB &c Ltd.
Copyright © 2018 FB &c Ltd.
FB &c Ltd, Dalton House, 60 Windsor Avenue, London, SW19 2RR.
Company number 08720141. Registered in England and Wales.

For support please visit www.forgottenbooks.com

1 MONTH OF FREE READING

at

www.ForgottenBooks.com

By purchasing this book you are eligible for one month membership to ForgottenBooks.com, giving you unlimited access to our entire collection of over 1,000,000 titles via our web site and mobile apps.

To claim your free month visit: www.forgottenbooks.com/free521842

* Offer is valid for 45 days from date of purchase. Terms and conditions apply.

English
Français
Deutsche
Italiano
Español
Português

www.forgottenbooks.com

Mythology Photography **Fiction**
Fishing Christianity **Art** Cooking
Essays Buddhism Freemasonry
Medicine **Biology** Music **Ancient Egypt** Evolution Carpentry Physics
Dance Geology **Mathematics** Fitness
Shakespeare **Folklore** Yoga Marketing
Confidence Immortality Biographies
Poetry **Psychology** Witchcraft
Electronics Chemistry History **Law**
Accounting **Philosophy** Anthropology
Alchemy Drama Quantum Mechanics
Atheism Sexual Health **Ancient History**
Entrepreneurship Languages Sport
Paleontology Needlework Islam
Metaphysics Investment Archaeology
Parenting Statistics Criminology
Motivational

A TRYAL OF WITCHES,

AT THE ASSIZES

HELD AT

BURY ST. EDMONDS

FOR THE

COUNTY OF SUFFOLK;

ON

THE TENTH DAY OF MARCH, 1664.

BEFORE

Sir Matthew Hale, Kt.

THEN

Lord Chief Baron of His Majestie's Court of Exchequer.

REPRINTED VERBATIM

FROM THE ORIGINAL EDITION OF 1682.

WITH AN APPENDIX

BY C. CLARK, ESQ., OF GREAT TOTHAM, ESSEX.

London:

JOHN RUSSELL SMITH,

4, OLD COMPTON STREET, SOHO.

1838.

GREENWICH:

PRINTED BY HENRY S. RICHARDSON,

STOCKWELL STREET.

TO THE READER.

This Tryal of Witches hath lain a long time in a private Gentleman's hands in the Country, it being given to him by the Person that took it in the Court for his own satisfaction; but it came lately to my hands, and having perused it, I found it a very remarkable thing, and fit to be Publish'd; especially in these times, wherein things of this nature are so much controverted, and that by persons of much Learning on both sides. I thought that so exact a Relation of this Tryal would probably give more satisfaction to a great many persons, by reason that it is pure Matter of Fact, and that evidently Demonstrated; than the Arguments and Reasons of other very Learned Men, that probably may not be so Intelligible to all Readers; especially, this being held before a Judge, whom for his Integrity, Learning, and Law, hardly any Age, either before or since could parellel; who not only took a great deal of paines, and spent much time in this Tryal himself; but had the Assistance and Opinion of several other very Eminent and Learned Persons: So that this being the most perfect Narrative of any thing of this Nature hitherto Extant, made me unwilling to deprive the World of the Benefit of it; which is the sole Motive that induced me to Publish it.

FAREWEL.

London, 1682.

A Tryal of Witches,

AT the Assizes and General Gaol delivery, held at Bury St. Edmonds for the County of Suffolk, the Tenth day of March, in the Sixteenth Year of the Reign of our Sovereign Lord King Charles II. before Matthew Hale, Knight, Lord Chief Baron of His Majesties Court of Exchequer; *Rose Cullender* and *Amy Duny*, Widows, both of Leystoff, in the County aforesaid, were severally indicted for Bewitching *Elizabeth* and *Ann Durent, Jane Bocking, Susan Chandler, William Durent, Elizabeth* and *Deborah Pacy*: And the said Cullender and Duny, being arraigned upon the said Indictments, pleaded NOT GUILTY: And afterwards, upon a long Evidence, were found GUILTY, and thereupon had Judgment to DYE for the same.

The Evidence whereupon these Persons were convicted of Witchcraft, stands upon divers particular Circumstances.

1. THREE of the Parties above-named, viz. Ann Durent, Susan Chandler, and Elizabeth Pacy, were brought to Bury to the Assizes and were in a reasonable good condition: But that Morning they came into the Hall to give Instructions for the drawing of their Bills of Indictments, the Three Persons fell into strange and violent fits, screeking out in a most sad manner, so that they could not in any wise give any Instructions in the Court who were the Cause of their Distemper. And although they did after some certain space recover out of their fits, yet they were every one of them struck Dumb, so that none of them could speak neither at that time, nor during the Assizes until the Conviction of the supposed Witches.

As concerning William Durent, being an Infant, his Mother Dorothy Durent sworn and examined deposed in open Court, That about the Tenth of March, *Nono Caroli Secundi*, she having a special occasion to go from home, and having none in her House to take care of her said Child (it then sucking) desired Amy Duny her Neighbour, to look to her Child during her absence, for which she promised her to give her a Penny: but the said Dorothy Durent desired the said Amy not to Suckle her Child, and laid a great charge upon her not to do it. Upon which it was asked by the Court, why she did give that direction, she being an old Woman and not capable of giving Suck? It was answered by the said Dorothy Durent, that she very well knew that she did not give Suck, but that for some years before, she had gone under the Reputation of a Witch, which was one cause made her give her the caution: Another was, That it was customary with old Women, that if they did look after a sucking Child, and nothing would please it but the Breast, they did use to please the Child to give it the Breast, and it did please the Child, but it sucked nothing but Wind, which did the Child hurt. Nevertheless after the departure of this Deponent, the said Amy did Suckle the Child: And after the return of the said Dorothy, the said Amy did acquaint her, That she had given Suck to the Child contrary to her command. Whereupon, the Deponent was very angry with the said Amy for the same; at which the said Amy was much discontented, and used many high Expressions and Threatning Speeches towards her; telling her, That she had as good to have done otherwise than to have found fault with her, and so departed out of her House: And that very Night her Son fell into strange fits of swounding, and was held in such terrible manner, that she was much affrighted therewith, and so continued for divers weeks. And the said Examinant farther said, that she being exceedingly troubled at her Childs Distemper, did go to a certain Person named Doctor Jacob, who lived at Yarmouth, who had the reputation in the Country, to help children that were Bewitch'd; who advis'd her to hang up the Childs Blanket in the Chimney-corner all day, and at night when she put the Child to Bed, to put it into the said blanket, and if she found anything in it, she should not be afraid, but to throw it into the Fire. And this Deponent did according to his direction; and at night when she took down the Blanket with an intent to put her Child therein, there fell out of the same a great T_{oad}, which ran up and down the hearth, and she having a young youth only with her in the House, desired him to catch the Toad, and throw it into the Fire, which the youth did accordingly, and held it there with the Tongs; and as soon as it was in the Fire it made a great and horrible Noise, and after a space there was a flashing in the Fire like Gun-powder, making a noise like the discharge of a Pistol, and thereupon the Toad was no more seen nor heard. It was asked by the Court, if that after the noise and flashing, there was not the Substance of the Toad to be seen to consume in the fire? And it was answered by the said Dorothy Durent, that after the flashing and noise, there was no more seen than if there had been none there. The next day there came a young Woman a Kinswoman of the said Amy, and a neighbour of this Deponent, and told this Deponent, that her Aunt (meaning the said Amy) was in a most lamentable condition having her face all scorched with fire, and that she was sitting alone in her House, in her smock without any fire. And thereupon this Deponent went into the House of the said Amy Duny to see her, and found her in the same condition as was related to her; for her Face, her Leggs, and Thighs, which this Deponent saw, seemed very much scorched and burnt with Fire, at which this Deponent seemed much to wonder. And asked the said Amy how she came into that sad condition? and the said Amy replied, she might thank her for it, for that she this Deponent was the cause thereof, but that she should live to see some of her Children dead, and she upon Crutches. And this Deponent farther saith, that after the burning of the said Toad, her Child recover'd, and was well again, and was living at the time of the Assizes. And this Deponent farther saith, That about the 6th. of March, 11° *Car.* 2. her Daughter Elizabeth Durent, being about the Age of Ten Years, was taken in like manner as her first Child was, and in her fits complained much of Amy Duny, and said, That she did appear to her, and Afflict her in such manner as the former. And she this Deponent going to the Apothecaries for some thing for her said Child, when she did return to her own House, she found the said Amy Duny there, and asked her what she did do there? and her answer was, That she came to see her Child, and to give it some water. But she this Deponent was very angry with her, and thrust her forth of her doors, and when she was out of doors, she said, You need not be so angry, for your Child will not live long: and this was on a Saturday, and the Child dyed on the Monday following. The cause of whose Death this Deponent verily believeth was occasion'd by the Witchcraft of the said Amy Duny: for that the said Amy hath been long reputed to be a Witch, and a person of very evil behaviour, whose Kindred and Relations have been many of them accused for Witchcraft, and some of them have been Condemned.

The said Deponent further saith, that not long after the death of her Daughter Elizabeth Durent, she this Deponent was taken with a Lameness in both her Leggs, from the knees downward, that she was fain to go upon Crutches, and that she had no other use of them but only to bear a little upon them till she did remove her Crutches, and so continued till the time of the Assizes, that the Witch came to be Tryed, and was there upon her Crutches; the Court asked her, That at the time she was taken with this Lameness, if it were with her according to the Custom of Women? Her Answer was, that it was so, and that she never had any stoppages of those things, but when she was with Child.

This is the Substance of her Evidence to this Indictment.

There was one thing very remarkable, that after she had gone upon Crutches for upwards of Three Years, and went upon them at the time of the Assizes in the Court when she gave her Evidence, and upon the Juries bringing in their Verdict, by which the said Amy Duny was found Guilty, to the great admiration of all Persons, the said Dorothy Durent was restored to the use of her Limbs, and went home without making use of her Crutches.

II. As concerning Elizabeth and Deborah Pacy, the first of the Age of Eleven Years, the other of the age of Nine Years or thereabouts: as to the Elder, she was brought into the Court at the time of the Instructions given to draw up the Indictments, and afterwards at the time of Tryal of the said Prisoners, but could not speak one Word all the time, and for the most part she remained as one wholly senseless as one in a deep Sleep, and could move no part of her body, and all the Motion of Life that appeared in her was, that as she lay upon Cushions in the Court upon her back, her stomack and belly by the drawing of her breath, would arise to a great height: and after the said Elizabeth had lain a long time on the Table in the Court, she came a little to her self and sate up, but could neither see nor speak, but was sensible of what was said to her, and after a while she laid her Head on the Bar of the Court with a Cushion under it, and her hand and her Apron upon that, and there she lay a good space of time: and by the direction of the Judge, Amy Duny was privately brought to Elizabeth Pacy, and she touched her hand; whereupon the Child without so much as seeing her, for her Eyes were closed all the while, suddenly leaped up, and catched Amy Duny by the hand, and afterwards by the face; and with her Nails scratched her till Blood came, and would by no means leave her till she was taken from her, and afterwards the Child would still be pressing towards her, and making signs of Anger conceived against her.

Deborah the younger Daughter was held in such extream manner, that her Parents wholly despaired of her life, and therefore could not bring her to the Assizes.

The Evidence which was given concerning these Two Children was to this Effect.

SAMUEL PACY a Merchant of Leystoff aforesaid, (a man who carried himself with much soberness during the Tryal, from whom proceeded no words either of Passion or Malice, though his Children were so greatly Afflicted,) Sworn and Examined, Deposeth, That his younger Daughter Deborah, upon Thursday the Tenth of October last, was suddenly taken with a Lameness in her Leggs, so that she could not stand, neither had she any strength in her Limbs to support her, and so she continued until the Seventeenth day of the same Month, which day being fair and Sunshiny, the Child desired to be carryed on the East part of the House, to be set upon the Bank which looketh upon the Sea; and whil'st she was sitting there, Amy Duny came to this Deponents House to buy some Herrings, but being denyed she went away discontented, and presently returned again, and was denyed, and likwise the third time and was denyed as at first; and at her last going away, she went away grumbling; but what she said was not perfectly understood. But at the very same instant of time, the said Child was taken with most violent fits, feeling most extream pain in her Stomach, like the pricking of Pins, and Shreeking out in a most dreadful manner, like unto a Whelp, and not like unto a sensible Creature. And in this extremity the Child continued to the great grief of the Parents until the Thirtieth of the same Month. During this time this Deponent sent for one Dr. Feavor, a Doctor of Physick, to take his advice concerning his Childs Distemper; the Doctor being come, he saw the Child in those fits, but could not conjecture (as he then told this Deponent, and afterwards affirmed in open Court, at this Tryal) what might be the cause of the Childs Affliction. And this Deponent farther saith, That by reason of the circumstances aforesaid, and in regard Amy Duny is a Woman of an ill Fame, and commonly reported to be a Witch and a Sorceress, and for that the said Child in her fits would cry out of Amy Duny as the cause of her Malady, and that she did affright her with Apparitions of her Person (as the Child in the intervals of her fits related) he this Deponent did suspect the said Amy Duny for a Witch, and charged her with the injury and wrong to his Child, and caused her to be set in the Stocks on the Twenty-eighth of the same October: and during the time of her continuance there, one Alice Letteridge and Jane Buxton demanding of her (as they also affirmed in Court upon their Oaths) what should be the reason of Mr. Pacy's Childs Distemper? telling her, That she was suspected to be the cause thereof; she replyed, Mr. Pacy keeps a great stir about his Child, but let him stay until he hath done as much by his Children, as I have done by mine. And being further examined, what she had done to her Children? She answered, That she had been fain to open her Child's Mouth with a Tap to give it Victuals.

And the said Deponent further deposeth, That within two days after speaking of the said words being the Thirtieth of October, the eldest Daughter Elizabeth, fell into extream fits, insomuch, that they could not open her Mouth to give her breath, to preserve her Life without the help of a Tap which they were enforced to use; and the younger Child was in the lil manner Afflicted, so that they used the same also for her Relief.

And further the said Children being grievously afflicted would severally complain in their extremity, and also in the intervals, That Amy Duny (together with one other Woman whose person and Cloathes they described) did thus Afflict them, their Apparitions appearing before them, to their great terrour and affrightment: And sometimes they would cry out, saying, There stands Amy Duny, and there Rose Cullender; the other Person troubling them.

Their fits were various, sometimes they would be lame on one side of their Bodies, sometimes on the other: sometimes a soreness over their whole Bodies, so as they could endure none to touch them: at other times they would be restored to the perfect use of their Limbs, and deprived of their Hearing; at other times of their Sight, at other times of their Speech; sometimes by the space of one day, sometimes for two; and once they were wholly deprived of their Speech for Eight days together, and then restored to their Speech again. At other times they would fall into Swoundings, and upon the recovery to their Speech they would Cough extreamly, and bring up much Flegme, and with the same crooked Pins, and one time a Two-penny Nail with a very broad head, which Pins (amounting to Forty or more) together with the Two-penny Nail were produced in Court, with the affirmation of the said Deponent, that he was present when the said Nail was Vomited up, and also most of the Pins. Commonly at the end of every fit they would cast up a Pin, and sometimes they would have four or five fits in one day.

In this manner the said Children continued with this Deponent for the space of two Months, during which time in their Intervals this Deponent would cause them to Read some

Chapters in the New Testament. Whereupon this Deponent several times observed, that they would read till they came to the Name of *Lord*, or *Jesus*, or *Christ;* and then before they could pronounce either of the said Words they would suddenly fall into their fits. But when they came to the Name of *Satan*, or *Devil*, they would clap their Fingers upon the Book, crying out, This bites, but makes me speak right well.

At such time as they be recovered out of their fits (occasion'd as this Deponent conceives upon their naming of *Lord*, or *Jesus*, or *Christ*,) this Deponent hath demanded of them, what is the cause they cannot pronounce those words, They reply and say, That Amy Duny saith, I must not use that name.

And farther, the said Children after their fits were past, would tell, how that Amy Duny, and Rose Cullender would appear before them, holding their Fists at them, threatning, That if they related either what they saw or heard, that they wo d Torment them Ten times more than ever they did before.

In their fits they would cry out, There stands Amy Duny, or Rose Cullender; and sometimes in one place and sometimes in another, running with great violence to the place where they fancied them to stand, striking at them as if they present; they would appear to them sometimes spinning, and sometimes reel-, ing, or in other postures, deriding or threatning them.

And this Deponent farther saith, That his Children being thus Tormented by all the space aforesaid, and finding no hopes of amendment, he sent them to his Sisters House, one Margaret Arnold, who lived at Yarmouth, to make tryal, whether the change of the Air might do them any good. And how, and in what manner they were afterwards held, he this Deponent refers himself to the Testimony of his said Sister.

Margaret Arnold, Sworn and Examined, saith, That the said Elizabeth and Deborah Pacy came to her House about the Thirtieth of November last, her Brother acquainted her, that he thought they were Bewitch'd, for that they vomited Pins; and farther Informed her of the several passages which occurred at his own House. This Deponent said, that she gave no credit to that which was related to her, conceiving possibly the Children might use some deceit in putting Pins in their mouths themselves. Wherefore this Deponent unpinned all their Cloathes, and left not so much as one Pin upon them, but sewed all the Cloathes they wore, instead of pinning of them: But this Deponent saith, that notwithstanding all this care and circumspection of hers, the Children afterwards raised at several times at least Thirty Pins in her presence, and had most fierce and violent Fitts upon them.

The Children would in their Fitts cry out against Rose Cullender and Amy Duny, affirming that they saw them; and they threatned to Torment them Ten times more, if they complained of them. At some times the Children (only) would see things run up and down the House in the appearance of Mice; and one of them suddainly snapt one with the Tongs, and threw it into the fire, and it screeched out like a Rat.

At another time, the younger Child being out of her Fitts went out of Doors to take a little fresh Air, and presently a little thing like a Bee flew upon her Face, and would have gone into her Mouth, whereupon the Child ran in all haste to the door to get into the House again, screeking out in a most terrible manner; whereupon, this Deponent made haste to come to her, but before she could get to her, the Child fell into her swooning Fitt, and at last with much pain straining herself, she vomitted up a Two-penny Nail with a broad Head; and after that the Child had raised up the Nail she came to her understanding; and being demanded by this Deponent, how she came by this Nail? she Answered, That the Bee brought this Nail and forced it into her Mouth.

And at other times, the Elder Child declared unto this Deponent, that during the time of her Fitts, she saw Flies come unto her, and bring with them in their Mouthes crooked Pins; and after the Child had thus declared the same, she fell again into violent Fits, and afterwards raised several Pins.

At another time, the said Elder Child declared unto this Deponent, and sitting by the Fire suddainly started up and said, she saw a Mouse, and she crept under the Table looking after it, and at lenght, she put something in her Apron, saying, she had caught it; and immediately she ran to the Fire and threw it in, and there did appear upon it to this Deponent, like the flashing of Gun-powder, though she confessed she saw nothing in the Childs Hand.

At another time the said Child being speechless, but otherwise, of perfect understanding, ran round about the House holding her Apron, crying hush, hush, as if there had been Poultrey in the House; but this Deponent could perceive nothing: but at last she saw the Child stoop as if she had catch't at something, and put it into her Apron, and afterwards made as if she had thrown it into the Fire: but this Deponent could not discover any thing: but the Child afterwards being restored to her speech, she this Deponent demanded of her what she saw at the time she used such a posture? who answered, That she saw a Duck.

At another time, the Younger daughter being recovered out of her Fitts, declared, That Amy Duny had been with her, and that she tempted her to Drown her self, and to cut her Throat, or otherwise to Destroy her self.

At another time, in their Fitts they both of them cryed out upon Rose Cullender and Amy Duny, complaining against them; Why do you not come your selves, but send your Imps to Torment us?

These several passages as most remarkable, the said Deponent did particularly set down as they daily happen'd, and for the reasons aforesaid, she doth verily believe in her conscience, that the Children were bewitched, and by the said Amy Duny, and Rose Cullender; though at first she could hardly be induced to believe it.

As concerning Ann Durent, one other of the Parties, supposed to be bewitched, present in Court.

Edmund Durent her Father Sworn and Examined; said, That he also lived in the said Town of Leystoff, and that the said Rose Cullender, about the latter end of November last, came into this Deponents House to buy some Herrings of his Wife, but being denyed by her, the said Rose returned in a discontented manner; and upon the first of December after, his Daughter Ann Durent was very sorely Afflicted in her Stomach, and felt great pain, like the pricking of Pins, and then fell into swooning fitts, and after the Recovery from her Fitts, she declared, That she had seen the Apparition of the said Rose, who threatned to Torment her. In this manner she continued from the first of December, until this present time of Tryal; having likewise vomited up divers Pins (produced here in Court.) This Maid was present in Court, but could not speak to declare her knowledge, but fell into most violent fits when she was brought before Rose Cullender.

Ann Baldwin Sworn and Examined, Deposeth the same thing as touching the Bewitching of the said Ann Durent.

As concerning Jane Bocking who was so weak, she could not be brought to the Assizes.

Diana Bocking Sworn and Examined, Deposed, That she lived in the same Town of Leystoff, and that her said Daughter having been formerly Afflicted with swooning fitts, recovered well of them, and so continued for a certain time; and upon the First of February last, she was taken also with great pain in her Stomach, like pricking with Pins; and afterwards fell into swooning fitts and so continued till the Deponents coming to the Assizes, having during the same time taken little or no food, but daily vomiting crooked Pins; and upon Sunday last raised Seven Pins. And whilst her fits were upon her she would spread forth her Arms with her hands open, and use postures as if she catched at something, and would instantly close her hands again; which being immediatly forced open, they found several Pins diversly crooked, but could neither see nor perceive how or in what manner they were conveyed thither. At another time, the same Jane being in another of her fitts, talked as if she were discoursing with some persons in the Room, (though she would give no answer nor seem to take notice of any person then present) and would in like manner cast abroad her Arms, saying, I will not have it, I will not have it; and at last she said, Then I will have it, and so waving her Arm with her hand open, she would presently close the same, which instantly forced open, they found in it a Lath-Nail. In her Fitts she would frequently complain of Rose Cullender and Amy Duny, saying, That now she saw Rose Cullender standing at the Beds feet, and another time at the Beds head, and so in other places. At last she was stricken Dumb and could not speak one Word, though her fitts were not upon her, and so she continued for some days, and at last her speech came to her again, and she desired her Mother to get her some Meat; and being demanded the reason why she could not speak in so long time? She answered, That Amy Duny would not suffer her to speak. This Lath-Nail, and divers of the Pins were produced in Court.

As concerning Susan Chandler, one other of the Parties supposed to be Bewitched and present in Court.

Mary Chandler Mother of the said Susan, Sworn and Examined, Deposed and said, That about the beginning of February last past, the said Rose Cullender and Amy Duny were Charged by Mr. Samuel Pacy for Bewitching of his Daughters. And a Warrant being granted at the request of the said Mr.

Pacy, by Sir Edmund Bacon, Baronet, one of the Justices of the Peace for the County of Suffolk, to bring them before him, and they being brought before him were Examined, and Confessed nothing. He gave order that they should be searched; whereupon this Deponent with five others were appointed to do the same: and coming to the House of Rose Cullender, they did acquaint her with what they were come about, and asked whether she was contented that they should search her? she did not oppose it, whereupon they began at her Head, and so stript her naked, and in the lower part of her Belly they found a thing like a Teat of an Inch long, they questioned her about it, and she said, That she had got a strain by carrying of water which caused that Excrescence. But upon narrower search, they found in her Privy Parts three more Excrescences or Teats, but smaller than the former: This Deponent farther saith, That in the long Teat at the end thereof there was a little hole, and it appeared unto them as if it had been lately sucked, and upon the straining of it there issued out white milkie Matter.

And this Deponent farther saith, That her said Daughter (being of the Age of Eighteen Years) was then in Service in the said Town of Leystoff, and rising up early the next Morning to Wash, this Rose Cullender appeared to her, and took her by the hand, whereat she was much affrighted, and went forthwith to her Mother, (being in the same town) and acquainted her with what she had seen; but being extreamly terrified, she fell extream sick, much grieved at her Stomach; and that Night after being in Bed with another young Woman, she suddenly scrieked out, and fell into such extream fits as if she were distracted, crying against Rose Cullender; saying, she would come to bed to her. She continued in this manner beating and wearing her self, insomuch, that this Deponent was glad to get help to attend her. In her Intervals she would declare, That some time she saw Rose Cullender, at another time with a great Dog with her: She also vomited up divers crooked Pins; and sometimes she was stricken with blindness, and at another time she was Dumb, and so she appeared to be in Court when the Tryal of the Prisoners was; for she was not able to speak her knowledge; but being brought into the Court at the Tryal, she suddenly fell into her fits, and being carryed out of the Court again, within the space of half an hour she came to her self and recovered her speech, and thereupon was immediatly brought into the Court, and asked by the Court, whether she was in condition to take an Oath, and to give Evidence, she said she could. But when she was Sworn, and asked what she could say against either of the Prisoners? before she could make any answer, she fell into her fits, screeking out in a miserable manner, crying Burn her, burn her, which were all the Words she could speak.

Robert Chandler, father of the said Susan, gave in the same Evidence, that his Wife Mary Chandler had given; only as to the searching of Rose Cullender as aforesaid.

This was the sum and Substance of the Evidence which was given against the Prisoners concerning the Bewitching of the Children before mentioned. At the hearing this Evidence there were divers known persons, as Mr. Serjeant Keeling, Mr. Serjeant Earl, and Mr. Serjeant Bernard, present. Mr. Serjeant Keeling seemed much unsatisfied with it, and thought it not sufficient to Convict the Prisoners: for admitting that the Children were in Truth Bewitched, yet said he, it can never be applyed to the Prisoners, upon the Imagination only of the Parties Afflicted; For if that might be allowed, no person whatsoever can be in safety, for perhaps they might fancy another person, who might altogether be innocent in such matters.

There was also Dr. Brown of Norwich, a Person of great knowledge; who after this Evidence given, and upon view of the three persons in Court, was desired to give his Opinion, what he did conceive of them: and he was clearly of Opinion, that the persons were Bewitched; and said, That in Denmark there had been lately a great Discovery of Witches, who used the very same way of Afflicting Persons, by conveying Pins into them, and crooked as these Pins were, with Needles and Nails. And his Opinion was, That the Devil in such cases did work upon the Bodies of Men and Women, upon a Natural Foundation, (that is) to stir up and excite such humours superabounding in their Bodies to a great excess, whereby he did in an extraordinary manner Afflict them with such Distempers as their Bodies were most subject to, as particularly appeared in these Children; for he conceived, that these swouning Fits were Natural, and nothing else but that they call the Mother, but only heightned to a great excess by the subtilty of the Devil, co-operating with the Malice of these which we term Witches, at whose Instance he doth these Villanies.

Besides the particulars above-mention'd touching the said persons Bewitched, there were many other things Objected against them for a further proof and manifestation that the said Children were Bewitched.

As First, during the time of the Tryal, there were some experiments made with the Persons Afflicted, by bringing the Persons to touch them; and it was observed, that when they were in the midst of their Fitts, to all Mens apprehension wholly deprived of all sense and understanding, closing their Fists in such manner, as that the strongest Man in the Court could not force them open; yet by the least touch of one of these supposed Witches, Rose Cullender by Name, they would suddenly shriek out opening their hands, which accident would not happen by the touch of any other person.

And least they might privately see when they were touched, by the said Rose Cullender, they were blinded with their own Aprons, and the touching took the same Effect as before.

There was an ingenious person that objected, there might be a great fallacy in this experiment, and there ought not to be any stress put upon this to Convict the Parties, for the Children might counterfeit this their Distemper, and perceiving what was done to them, they might in such manner suddenly alter the motion and gesture of their Bodies, on purpose to induce persons to believe that they were not natural, but wrought strangely by the touch of the Prisoners.

Wherefore to avoid this scruple it was privately desired by the Judge, that the Lord Cornwallis, Sir Edmund Bacon, and Mr. Serjeant Keeling, and some other Gentlemen there in Court, would attend one of the Distempered persons in the farther part of the Hall, whilst she was in her fits, and then to send for one of the Witches, to try what would then happen, which they did accordingly: and Amy Duny was conveyed from the Bar and brought to the Maid: they put an Apron before her Eyes, and then one other person touched her hand, which produced the same effect as the touch of the Witch did in the Court. Whereupon the Gentlemen returned, openly protesting, that they did believe the whole transaction of this business was a meer Imposture.

This put the Court and all persons into a stand. But at length Mr. Pacy did declare, That possibly the Maid might be deceived by a suspition that the Witch touched her when she did not. For he had observed divers times, that although they could not speak, but were deprived of the use of their Tongues and Limbs, that their understandings were perfect, for that they have related divers things which have been when they were in their fits, after they were recovered out of them. This saying of Mr. Pacy was found to be true afterwards, when his Daughter was fully recovered (as she afterwards was) as shall in due time be related: For she was asked, whither she did hear and understand any thing that was done and acted in the

Court, during the time that she lay as one deprived of her understanding? and she said, she did: and by the Opinions of some, this experiment, (which others would have a Fallacy) was rather a confirmation that the Parties were really Bewitched, than otherwise: for say they, it is not possible that any should counterfeit such Distempers, being accompanied with such various Circumstances, much less Children; and for so long time, and yet undiscovered by their Parents and Relations: For no man can suppose that they should all Conspire together, (being out of several families, and, as they Affirm, no way related one to the other, and scarce of familiar acquaintance) to do an Act of this nature whereby no benefit or advantage could redound to any of the Parties, but a guilty Conscience for Perjuring themselves in taking the Lives of two poor simple Women away, and there appears no Malice in the Case. For the Prisoners themselves did scarce so much as Object it. Wherefore, say they, it is very evident that the Parties were Bewitched, and that when they apprehend or understand by any means, that the persons who have done them this wrong are near, or touch them; then their spirits being more than ordinarily moved with rage and anger at them being present, they do use more violent gestures of their Bodies, and extend forth their hands, as desirous to lay hold upon them; which at other times not having the same occasion, the instance there falls not out the same.

2ly. One John Soam of Leystoff aforesaid, Yeoman, a sufficient Person, Deposeth, That not long since, in harvest time he had three Carts which brought home his Harvest, and as they were going into the Field to load, one of the Carts wrenched the Window of Rose Cullenders House, whereupon she came out in a great rage and threatned this Deponent for doing that wrong, and so they passed along into the Fields and loaded all the Three Carts, the other two Carts returned safe home, and back again, twice loaded that day afterwards; but as to this Cart which touched Rose Cullenders House, after it was loaded, it was overturned twice or thrice that day; and after that they had loaded it again the second or third time, as they brought it through the Gate which leadeth out of the Field into the Town, the Cart stuck so fast in the Gateshead, that they could not possibly get it through, but were inforced to cut down the Post of the Gate to make the Cart pass through, although they could not perceive that the Cart did of either side touch the Gate-posts. And this Deponent further saith, That after they had got it through the Gate-way, they did with much difficulty get it home into the Yard; but for all that they could do, they could not get the Cart near unto the place where they should unload the Corn, but were fain to unload it at a great distance from the place, and when they began to unload they found much difficulty therein, it being so hard a labour that they were tired that first came; and when others came to assist them, their Noses burst forth a bleeding: so they were fain to desist and leave it until the next Morning, and then they unloaded it without any difficulty at all.

Robert Sherringham also Deposeth against Rose Cullender, That about Two Years since, passing along the Street with his Cart and Horses, the Axletree of his Cart touched her House, and broke down some part of it, at which, she was very much displeased, threatning him, that his Horses should suffer for it; and so it happen'd, for all those Horses, being Four in Number, died within a short time after: since that time he hath had great Losses by the suddain dying of his other Cattle; so soon as his Sows pigged, the Pigs would leap and caper, and immediately fall down and dye. Also, not long after, he was taken with a Lameness in his Limbs that he could neither go nor stand for some days. After all this, he was very much vexed with great Number of Lice of an extraordinary bigness, and although he many times shifted himself, yet he was not any thing the better, but would swarm again with them; so that in the Conclusion he was forc'd to burn all his Clothes, being two suits of Apparel, and then was clean from them.

As concerning Amy Duny, one Richard Spencer Deposeth, That about the first of September last, he heard her say at his House, That the Devil would not let her rest until she were Revenged on one Cornelius Sandeswell's Wife.

Ann Sandeswell, Wife unto the above-said Cornelius, Deposed, That about Seven or Eight Years since, she having bought a certain number of Geese, meeting with Amy Duny, she told her, If she did not fetch her Geese home they would all be Destroyed: which in a few days after came to pass.

Afterwards the said Amy became Tenant to this Deponents Husband for a House, who told her, That if she looked not well to such a Chimney in her House, that the same would fall: Whereupon this Deponent replyed, That it was a new one; but not minding much her Words, at that time they parted. But in a short time the Chimney fell down according as the said Amy had said.

Also this Deponent farther saith, That her Brother being a Fisherman, and using to go into the Northern Seas, she desired him to send her a Firkin of Fish, which he did accordingly; and she having notice that the said Firkin was brought into Leystoff-Road, she desired a Boatman to bring it ashore with the other Goods they were to bring; and she going down to meet the Boat-man to receive her Fish, desired the said Amy to go along with her to help her home with it; Amy Replyed, She would go when she had it. And thereupon this Deponent went to the Shoar without her, and demanded of the Boat-man the Firkin, they told her, That they could not keep it in the Boat from falling into the Sea, and they thought it was gone to the Devil, for they never saw the like before. And being demanded by this Deponent, whether any other Goods in the Boat were likewise lost as well as hers? They answered, Not any.

This was the substance of the whole Evidence given against the Prisoners at the Bar; who being demanded what they had to say for themselves? They replyed, Nothing material to any thing that was proved against them. Whereupon the Judge in giving his direction to the Jury, told them, That he would not repeat the Evidence unto them, least by so doing he should wrong the Evidence on the one side or on the other. Only this acquainted them, That they had Two things to enquire after. First, Whether or no these Children were Bewitched? Secondly, Whether the Prisoners at the Bar were Guilty of it?

That there were such Creatures as Witches he made no doubt at all; For First, the Scriptures had affirmed so much. Secondly, The wisdom of all Nations had provided Laws against such Persons, which is an Argument of their confidence of such a Crime. And such hath been the judgment of this Kingdom, as appears by that Act of Parliament which hath provided Punishments proportionable to the quality of the Offence. And desired them, strictly to observe their Evidence; and desired the great God of Heaven to direct their Hearts in this weighty thing they had in hand: For to Condemn the Innocent, and to let the Guilty go free, were both an Abomination to the Lord.

With this short Direction the Jury departed from the Bar, and within the space of half an hour returned, and brought them in both *GUILTY* upon the several Indictments, which were Thirteen in Number, whereupon they stood Indicted.

This was upon Thursday in the Afternoon, March 13, 1664.

The next Morning, the Three Children with their Parents came to the Lord Chief Baron Hale's Lodging, who all of them spake perfectly, and were as in good Health as ever they were; only Susan Chandler, by reason of her very much Affliction, did look very thin and wan. And their friends were asked, At what time they were restored thus to their Speech and Health? And Mr. Pacy did Affirm, That within less than half an hour after the Witches were Convicted, they were all of them Restored, and slept well that Night, feeling no pain; only Susan Chandler felt a pain like pricking of Pins in her Stomach.

After, they were all of them brought down to the Court, but Ann Durent was so fearful to behold them, that she desired she might not see them. The other Two continued in the Court, and they Affirmed in the face of the Country, and before the Witches themselves, what before hath been Deposed by their Friends and Relations; the Prisoners not much contradicting them. In Conclusion, the Judge and all the Court were fully satisfied with the Verdict, and thereupon gave Judgment against the Witches that they should be Hanged.

They were much urged to confess, but would not.

That morning we departed for Cambridge, but no Reprieve was granted: And they were Executed on Monday, the Seventeenth of March following, but they Confessed nothing.

END OF THE TRIAL.

Appendix.

A Witch, according to old descriptions, was generally blessed with a " wrinkled face, a furred brow, a hairy lip, a gobber tooth, a squint eye, a squeaking voice, a scolding tongue, a ragged coat on her back, a scull-cap on her head, a spindle in her hand, and a dog or cat by her side;" and Lord Coke pithily describes a " Witch to be a person that hath conference with the devil, to consult with him or to do some act." In former times the most eminent men and philosophers (Sir Thomas Brown for instance.—See p. 16) were not proof against the prevailing opinions. A modern writer observes, that one would imagine that the establishment of Protestanism would have conduced to the abolition of this lamentable and pernicious credulity. But the Reformation did not arrive with great rapidity at its full extent, and the belief in Witchcraft long continued to "overspread the land." Indeed it has been proved by Hutchinson, in his *Essay on Witchcraft*, that the change of religion at first rather augmented than diminished the evil. A degree of importance, hardly credible in these times, was attached to it; and in the sixteenth century the unbelievers were accounted " Sadducees, Atheists, and Infidels !" One of the most eminent divines of the day, a strenuous advocate in the belief of Witchcraft, characterises them thus in the most forcible language! It is not surprising, therefore, that the supposed dabblers in the infernal art were hunted out and exposed to the most dreadful cruelty and oppression, not only from those who imagined they had suffered under their charms, but from the very laws of the realm also. The first trial of any note took place in 1593. Three persons, old Samuel and his wife and daughter Agnes, were condemned at Huntingdon, before Mr. Justice Fenner, for bewitching a Mr. Throgmorton's family, &c. A few years after, an advocate for this belief appeared from no less a quarter than the throne itself. King James I. in his *Demonologie*, completely superseded Reginald Scot's *Discoverie of Witchcraft*, a work which completely unmasked the whole machinery, and was a storehouse of facts on the subject. The infection, commenced at the throne, soon reached the Parliament, and (as it has been observed the greatest part of mankind have no other reason for their opinions than that they are in fashion) a statute was passed in the first year of King James, having for its object, as expressed in the preamble, "the more effectual punishment of those detestable slaves of the devil, witches, sorcerers, enchanters, and conjurors." The punishment was enacted to be the pillory for the first offence (even though its object were not effected) and death for the second. "Thus was the detestable doctrine established both by law and fashion, and it became not only unpolite but criminal to doubt it; and, as prodigies are always seen in proportion as they are expected, witches were every day discovered, and multiplied so fast in some places, that Bishop Hall mentions a village in Lancashire where their number was greater than that of the houses." There was dreadful havoc in that county after this law had passed. Lancashire has always been remarkable for the number of its witches. Though the information we have to go upon cannot, of course, be considered as very accurate, yet it has been ascertained that between the commencement of the statute in question (1602) and the year 1701, in the space of one century, 3192 persons were executed for the crimes of Witchcraft and Sorcery! The act alluded to was rigorously enforced during this period, and the above calculation is probably under the mark, and does not include the numbers that were tried on suspicion, but acquitted for want of sufficient proof of the charges alleged against them.

WITCHCRAFT IN SUFFOLK. In 1644, one Matthew Hopkins, of Manningtree, in Essex, who styled himself *Witch-finder General*, and had 20s. allowed him for every town he visited, was, with some others, commissioned by Parliament to perform a circuit for the discovery of witches, during this and the two following years. Thus authorised, they went from place to place, through many parts of Suffolk, Norfolk, and Huntingdonshire; but what appears still more astonishing, they caused 16 persons to be hanged at Yarmouth, 40 at Bury, and others in different parts of the county to the amount of 60 persons!! Butler, in his *Hudibras*, alludes to this when he makes his hero say—

> "Has not this present Parliament
> A ledger to the devil sent,
> Fully empowered to treat about
> Finding revolted witches out?
> And has not he within one year
> Hang'd threescore of them in a shire?"

A Mr. Lowes, an innocent and aged clergyman, vicar of Brandeston, was among the victims sacrificed by this impostor and his associates. A cooper and his wife, and fifteen other women, were by the same influence all condemned and executed at one time at Bury! Besides the arts used by Hopkins to extort confession from suspected persons, he had recourse to *swimming them;* which was done by tying their thumbs and great toes together, previously to throwing them into the water: if they sunk it was a proof of their innocence, but if they floated they were guilty. This method he pursued till some gentlemen, indignant at his barbarity, tied his own thumbs and toes, as he had been accustomed to tie those of other persons, and when put into the water, he himself swam, as many others had done before him. By this expedient the country was cleared of him. *Hudibras* alludes to this when, speaking of Hopkins, he says—

"Who after proved himself a witch,
And made a rod for his own breech."

The following curious Letter is copied from a manuscript in the British Museum:—

"From Mr. Manning, Dissenting Teacher, at Halstead, in Essex, to John Morley, Esq., Halstead.

"Halstead, Aug. 2, 1732.

"SIR,—The narrative which I gave you in relation to witchcraft, and which you are pleased to lay your commands upon me to repeat, is as follows:—There was one master Collett, a smith by trade, of Haveningham, in the County of Suffolk, who, as 'twas customary with him, assisting the maide to churne, and not being able (as the phrase is) to make the butter come, threw a hot iron into the churn, under the notion of witchcraft in the case, upon which a poore labourer, then employéd in carrying of dung in the yard, cried out in a terrible manner, 'they have killed me, they have killed me;' still keeping his hand upon his back, intimating where the pain was, and died upon the spot.

"Mr. Collett, with the rest of the servants then present, took off the poor man's clothes, and found to their great surprise, the mark of the iron that was heated and thrown into the churn, deeply impressed upon his back. This account I had from Mr. Collett's own mouth, who being a man of unblemished character, I verily believe to be matter of fact.

"I am, Sir, your obliged humble servant,
"SAM. MANNING."

An old gentleman, who died at Polstead, in Suffolk, some years ago, lamented till his death a sight he had lost when a boy, only for the want of five pounds; a man having undertaken for that sum to make all the witches in the parish dance on the knoll together; and though he grew up a penurious man, and lived a bachelor till fifty, he never ceased to lament that such an opportunity of seeing these weird-sisters collected together, never occurred again. He used to say he had seen a witch *swam* on Polstead Ponds, and "she went over the water like a cork." He had, when a boy, stopped a wizard on his way to Stoke, by laying a line of single straws across the path; and, concealed in a hedge, he had watched an old woman (alias witch) feeding her imps in the form of three blackbirds.

WITCH-FINDING AT NEWCASTLE.—Mention occurs of a petition in the common council books of Newcastle, dated March 26th, 1649, and signed, no doubt, by the inhabitants, concerning witches, the purport of which appears, from what followed, to have occasioned all such persons as were suspected, to be apprehended and brought to trial. In consequence of this, the magistrates sent two of their serjeants into Scotland, to agree with a Scotchman, who pretended knowledge to find out witches by pricking them with pins, to come to Newcastle, where he should try such as should be brought to him, and have twenty shillings a-piece for all he should condemn as witches, and free passage thither and back. When the serjeants brought the witch-finder on horseback to town, the magistrates sent their bellman through the town, ringing his bell and crying, all people that would bring in any complaint against any woman for a witch, they should be sent for, and tried by the person appointed. Thirty women were brought into the Town Hall, and had pins thrust into their flesh, and most of them were found guilty.—It appears by an extract from the registry of the parochial chapelry of St. Andrews, in Scotland, that one man and fifteen women were executed at Newcastle for witchcraft; and there is a print of this horrid execution in *Gardner's England's Grievance Discovered*, 1655, reprinted at Newcastle, 1796.—When the witch-finder had done in Newcastle, and received his wages, he went into Northumberland, to try women there, and got £3. a-piece; but Henry Ogle, Esq., laid hold on him, and required bond of him, to answer at the sessions. He escaped into Scotland, where he was made prisoner, indicted, arraigned, and condemned for such-like villany exercised in Scotland, and confessed at the gallows that he had been the death of above 220 women in England and Scotland, for the gain of 20*s*. a-piece!!—*Sykes's Local Records*.

WITCHCRAFT IN LANCASHIRE.—In 1634, seventeen Pendle-forest witches were condemned in Lancashire, by the infamous contrivances of a boy only eleven years of age, and his father. Amongst other charges equally wonderful and miraculous, this little villain deposed that a greyhound was transformed by their agency into "one Dickenson's wife," &c. These poor creatures, however, obtained a reprieve, and were sent to London, where they first viewed and examined by his majesty's physicians and surgeons, and then by "*his majesty himself and the council.*" The result was that the boy's contrivances were exposed and properly punished. In 1664, Alice Hudson, who was burnt at York, said she received money from the devil, ten shillings at a time!

ORIGIN OF WALTZING.—The origin of that elegant accomplishment, *waltzing*, is derived from the orgies of the devils and witches during the ceremony of initiation, who on these occasions never failed to dance. Each had a broomstick in her hand, and held it up aloft. "*Also that these night-walking, or rather night-dancing, devils brought out of Italy into France that dance which is called La Volta.*"—See Bodin in his *Lib. de Demonomania*, and Scot's *Discoverie*. This is certainly the origin of the modern waltz; and that it should take its derivation from so diabolical a source is much to be lamented. Some, however, have endeavoured to trace the waltz from certain feasts of Bacchus, called *Orgia*.

WITCHCRAFT IN ESSEX.—About the year 1576, seventeen or eighteen persons were condemned for witchcraft at St. Osyth, in Essex. An account of them was written by Brian Darcy, with the names and colours of their spirits!—*See Scot's Discovery.*

In 1645, fifteen persons were condemned for witchcraft at Chelmsford, and hanged—some at Chelmsford and some at Manningtree. Another died in gaol. Another died as going to execution. They were condemned at a Sessions by the Earl of Warwick, and some Justices of the Peace.—*Hutchinson's Essay.*

About half a century ago, the inhabitants of the rural village of Great Totham, Essex, were witnesses of one of those strange ceremonies, the swimming of a person who was suspected to be a witch. From a person who was present and saw the whole of the proceedings, and upon whose veracity I can rely, I have collected the following particulars:—At an old cottage, a part of which is still standing, situate on the western side of Totham Hill, to the right of the road leading to Beckingham, dwelt an old widow-woman of rather singular habits of the name of Scotcher. One morning in harvest time, she and her daughter, who, with her husband, lived with her, were found by one Master Fitch, a small farmer at Great Totham, who happened to be accompanied that morning by the village blacksmith, a person of the name of Acers, in one of the fields of the former, gleaning,—it being but just light, and a much earlier hour than the rest of the inhabitants were accustomed to go out into the fields to glean. On being told that they had no right to be there at that time of the morning, and ordered to leave the field, they were much offended, and Scotcher became very abusive. At length, finding that words would not prevail, Acers went and procured a hedge-stake, and, assisted by Fitch, drove them out of the field by force. Acers used his weapon only *in terrorem;* but after they had driven them out of the field, being much excited by their conduct, he seized hold of both the offenders, and knocked their heads together with great force, telling Scotcher that she was a Witch, and that he would have her swam. This threat was actually put into execution a few days after, in the presence of a great number of the villagers, at "Totham Pond," (now laid dry and cultivated,) situate by the side of the road leading from Maldon to Colchester. The suspected witch, after having been stript of all her habiliments save her under garment, her feet and hands confined together, and a rope tied round her waist, to enable the officiating person to pull her out of the water again, if they found she was in danger of drowning, was put into a large tub, where she was received by Acers, who, all being arranged, immediately shoved the tub from the side, and continued floating it until they had got to the deepest part of the pond, when he threw her into the water, and—*she swam!* Although she tried all she could, and even "dived down into the water like a duck," said my informant, "she could no more sink than a piece of cork!" After she had been worried about in the water for some time, she was taken out and allowed to depart; those assembled being quite satisfied that she was one of those "slaves of the Devil," yclept a Witch!

According to Strype, Bishop Jewel, preaching before the Queen, in 1558, said: "It may please your grace to understand that witches and sorcerers, within these few last years, are marvelously increased within your grace's realm. Your grace's subjects pine away, even unto the death, their colour fadeth, their flesh rotteth, their speech is benumbed, their senses are bereft. I pray God they never practice *further than upon the subject.*" "This," says Strype, "I make no doubt was the occasion of bringing in a bill, the next parliament, for making enchantments and witchcraft felony." One of the bishop's strong expressions is, "These eyes have seen most evident and manifest marks of their wickedness."

In Archbishop Cranmer's Articles of Visitation, 1549, is the following:—"*Item*, You shall enquire, whether you know of any that use charms, sorcery, enchantments, witchcraft, soothsaying, or any like craft, invented by the Devil."

John Bell, minister of the gospel at Glaidsmuir, says:—
"Providently, two tests appeared to discover the crime: if the witch cries out 'Lord, have mercy upon me!' when apprehended; and the inability of shedding tears: because, as a witch could only shed three tears, and those with her left eye, her stock was quickly exhausted; and that was the more striking, as King James I. shrewdly observes, 'since other women in general are like the crocodile, ready to weep upon every slight occasion.

About the year 1679, a witch was condemned at Ely, but reprieved by King Charles II., and afterwards the fellow that pretended to have been bewitched, was hanged at Chelmsford, in Essex, and confessed that he had counterfeited his fits and vomitings.—*Hutchinson's Essay.*

In 1716, Mrs. Hicks, and her daughter aged *nine*, were hanged at Huntingdon for selling their souls to the Devil, and raising a storm, by pulling off their stockings and making a lather of soap! With this crowning atrocity, the catalogue of murders in England closes; the penal statutes against witchcraft being repealed in 1736, and the pretended exercise of such arts being punished in future by imprisonment and pillory. Barrington, in his observations on the statute 20 Henry VI., does not hesitate to estimate the numbers of those put to death in England on the charge of witchcraft at 30,000!—*Foreign Quarterly Review.*

Valuable and Interesting Books

PUBLISHED OR SOLD BY

JOHN RUSSELL SMITH,

4, OLD COMPTON STREET, SOHO SQUARE, LONDON.

A DICTIONARY of ARCHAIC and PROVINCIAL WORDS, OBSOLETE PHRASES, PROVERBS, and ANCIENT CUSTOMS, from the XIVth Century. Forming a Key to the Writings of our Ancient Poets, Dramatists, and other Authors, whose works abound with allusions of which explanations are not to be found in the ordinary books of reference. By JAMES ORCHARD HALLIWELL, F.R.S., F.S.A., &c. 8vo. Parts I. and II. *closely printed in double columns, 2s. 6d. each.*
⁎ To be completed in Twelve Parts.

The work now placed before the notice of the public is intended to furnish a Manual, the want of which has long been felt by most persons who have had occasion to study or refer to the works of our old writers. No general dictionary of the early English language has hitherto appeared, and the student often finds himself at a loss, when, probably, a comprehensive glossary would at once give the information required. To remedy this inconvenience, the present publication has been projected. It is intended, within as moderate a compass as possible, to give a large collection of those obsolete and provincial words which are most likely to be generally useful, without extending the size and cost of the work by etymological or other similar researches; and while care is taken to establish, as far as possible, the correct meanings of the words, to avoid discussions on subjects that would be interesting only to the professed etymologist. It is not, of course, proposed to exclude etymology, but merely to render it subservient in the way of explanation, and not allow it to occupy much space. Bearing this general plan always in view, it is hoped that the work, when completed, will be found a useful book of reference in the hands of a large class of readers. Most of the principal archaisms will be illustrated by examples, many of them selected from early inedited MSS. and rare books, and by far the larger portion will be found to be original authorities. The libraries of Lincoln, Cambridge, and Oxford have supplied much valuable material for this purpose. Without examples it is often difficult to convey the true meaning, and the references to books more readily accessible will enable the student to pursue the history of any particular word to a greater extent than our plan has here permitted.

"This promises to be a most useful work ... Mr. Halliwell, though habitually too off-handed to be altogether satisfactory, is, we must acknowledge, as well qualified, by industry, ability, and previous study, to be the editor as any man living. We could indeed easily name a dozen persons, each of whom would be better qualified for particular departments, but not one who, including the whole range embraced by the title, would have the ability and energy to go through all the drudging duties of the office more satisfactorily. It is a work, however, that, in the first instance, must be imperfect. We hold, therefore, that every English scholar should have an interleaved copy, that he may contribute a something towards improving a second edition. The first number appears to have been carefully compiled; but we are not inclined to seek very curiously for faults in a work of such obvious difficulty, when, even if it be imperfect, it cannot fail to be useful."—*Athenæum.*

NURSERY RHYMES of ENGLAND, collected chiefly from Oral Tradition. Edited by JAMES ORCHARD HALLIWELL, Esq. F.R.S. The THIRD EDITION, with alterations and additions, royal 18mo, with 33 Designs by W. B. Scott, engraved by Orrin Smith and Linton, extra cloth, 4s. 6d.

"Well done! 'Third Edition!' Q. What could make a collection of nursery rhymes more than ever acceptable to the large and small public? A. Illustrations. And here they are: clever pictures, which the three-year olds understand before their A, B, C, and which the fifty-three-year olds like almost as well as the threes."—Lit. Gaz.

"We paid a merited tribute to the former editions of this collection. The present volume with its neat and droll little vignettes, is reduced to dimensions such as to render it not too bulky for that important part of the public who are the most legitimate and numerous patrons of Nursery Rhymes."—Globe.

"We confess to a sort of respect for these Nursery Rhymes, when we consider that they were sung to the rocking of the cradles of such people as Milton and Shakspeare, and Locke and Newton, and we are therefore well pleased to see them collected into an erudite volume, one, too, that may be useful to the antiquary, by helping him to trace the footprints of the backward steps of time."—Metropolitan Magazine.

"Not only all mothers, aunts, nurses (for nurses can even read now) are obliged to Mr. Halliwell for this careful and elegant collection of this most popular portion of our national poetry, but grave and gray-head scholars may find in them traces of manners long passed away, and sentiments that may awaken a pleasing train of meditations."
Monthly Magazine.

"We are persuaded that the very rudest of these jingles, tales, and rhymes possess a strong imagination-nourishing power; and that in infancy and early childhood a sprinkling of ancient nursery lore is worth whole cartloads of the wise saws and modern instances which are now as duly and carefully concocted by experienced litterateurs into instructive tales for the *spelling* public, as are works of entertainment for the reading public. The work is worthy of the attention of the popular antiquary."—Tait's Mag. Feb. 1843.

*** The public are cautioned against other works with imitative titles, which have been published since the second edition of the above, and which are mostly *pirated* from it. Mr. Halliwell's is the cheapest and most copious book.

AUTOBIOGRAPHY of JOSEPH LISTER, of Bradford, in Yorkshire, to which is added a cotemporary account of the Defence of Bradford and Capture of Leeds by the Parliamentarians in 1642. Edited by THOMAS WRIGHT, M.A. F.S.A. &c. 8vo, cloth, 4s. [ONLY 250 COPIES PRINTED.]

"This volume is curious in several respects: 1st, as showing us the spirit, tenets, and manners of the nonconformists; 2dly, as minutely describing some remarkable affairs belonging to the civil wars; and 3dly, as throwing a light upon the general habits of a particular class of the inhabitants of England two hundred years ago."—Literary Gaz.

"Several remarkable matters may be collected from its perusal, and such compositions are always valuable as pictures of character and manners."—Gent's Mag.

"The volume is a curious and interesting fragment of the history of those eventful times. It gives a welcome glimpse of the early nonconformists."—Bradford Observer.

LOVE LETTERS of MRS. PIOZZI, written when she was Eighty, to the handsome Actor, WILLIAM AUGUSTUS CONWAY, aged Twenty-seven. 8vo, sewed, 2s.

"—— written at three, four, and five o'clock (in the morning) by an Octogenary pen, a heart (as Mrs. Lee says) twenty-six years old, and as H. L. P. feels it to be, *all your own*."—Letter V. 3d Feb. 1820.

"This is one of the most extraordinary collections of love epistles we have ever chanced to meet with, and the well known literary reputation of the lady—the Mrs. Thrale, of Dr. Johnson and Miss Burney celebrity—considerably enhances their interest. The letters themselves it is not easy to characterize; nor shall we venture to decide whether they more bespeak the drivelling of dotage or the folly of love; in either case they present human nature to us under a new aspect, and furnish one of those riddles which nothing yet dreamt of in our philosophy can satisfactorily solve."—Polytechnic Rev.

ENGLISH SURNAMES. A Series of Essays on Family Nomenclature, Historical, Etymological, and Humorous; with Chapters on Canting Arms, Rebuses, the Roll of Battel Abbey, a List of Latinized Surnames, &c. By MARK ANTONY LOWER. The SECOND EDITION, ENLARGED, post 8vo, pp. 292, with 20 woodcuts, cloth, 6s.

" This is a curious volume, and full of divers matter, which comes home to everybody, both in the way of information and amusement."—*Literary Gazette.*

" This is a curious book of its kind, written by a man of some antiquarian reading, and possessed of a certain vein of dry humour. He apologizes to the utilitarian for the frivolity of his subject; but the origin of surnames is a branch of the history of the formation of language, and of the natural operations of the mind in making known or supplying its wants...... Taken, as a whole, the book is really entertaining as well as informing."—*Tait's Mag.*

" An instructive and amusing volume, which ought to be popular. Perhaps no subject is more curious than the history of proper names. How few persons are there who have not on one occasion or other been struck with the singular names which have fallen under their own observation, and who have not sought for information as to their origin? Yet we know of no work of any value, much more a popular work, which treats on the subject. Mr. Lower has written a very good and well-arranged book, which we can with confidence recommend to our readers."—*Archæologist.*

" This is a most amusing volume, mingling wit and pleasantry with antiquarian research and historical interest."—*Weekly Chronicle.*

ST. PATRICK'S PURGATORY: an Essay on the Legends of Purgatory, Hell, and Paradise, current during the Middle Ages. By THOMAS WRIGHT, M.A., F.S.A., &c. Post 8vo, cloth, 6s.

" It must be observed, that this is not a mere account of St. Patrick's Purgatory, but a complete history of the legends and superstitions relating to the subject, from the earliest times, rescued from old MSS. as well as from old printed books. Moreover, it embraces a singular chapter of literary history, omitted by Warton and all former writers with whom we are acquainted; and we think we may add, that it forms the best introduction to Dante that has yet been published."—*Literary Gazette.*

" This appears to be a curious and even amusing book on the singular subject of purgatory, in which the idle and fearful dreams of superstition are shown to be first narrated as tales, and then applied as means of deducing the moral character of the age in which they prevailed."—*Spectator.*

" This is a very curious and learned work, and must have cost the writer an immense deal of research. The subject is full of interest, and one on which we have scarcely any literature, at least in a collected form. It is a curious fact, that nearly all the old monkish legends relative to purgatory are either English or Irish. They are exceedingly poetical, and open up a new field to the imaginative mind. There can be no estimation of the power these Legends must have had upon the minds of the ignorant people of the middle ages. The monks, when they invented them, perfectly knew what they were about, and perhaps they did what was best on the whole,—they could only reach the intellect of the age by these means."—*Weekly Chronicle.*

Dramatic Literature.

A COURSE of LECTURES on DRAMATIC ART and LITERATURE. By AUGUSTUS WILLIAM SCHLEGEL. Translated from the German by JOHN BLACK, Esq., Editor of the ' Morning Chronicle.' 2 vols. foolscap 8vo. SECOND EDITION, cloth, 12s.

" The present work contains a critical and historical account of the ancient and modern drama—the Greek, Latin, Italian, German, Spanish, and English. The view which the author has taken of the standard productions, whether tragic or comic, is ingenious and just, and his reasonings on the principles of taste are as satisfactory as they are profound. The acute and sensible remarks—the high tone of morality—are very admirable and exemplary; and we refer those who desire to elevate their understandings to a guide so learned and philosophical as the author of these volumes."—*Edinb. Rev.*

" In a few pages we reap the fruit of the labour of a whole life. Every opinion formed by the author, every epithet given to the writers of whom he speaks is beautiful and just, concise and animated."—*Mad. de Stael's Germany.*

" A work of extraordinary merit."—*Quarterly Review,* Vol. XII. pp. 112-46.

SHAKESPERIANA, a Catalogue of the Early Editions of Shakespeare's Plays, and of the Commentaries and other Publications illustrative of his Works. By JAMES ORCHARD HALLIWELL, Esq. F.R.S. F.S.A. &c. 8vo, *cloth*, 3s.

"Indispensable to everybody who wishes to carry on any inquiries connected with Shakespeare, or who may have a fancy for Shakesperian Bibliography."—*Spectator.*

"It ought to be placed by the side of every edition. It is the most concise, yet the most copious illustration of the subject which has been given to the public."—*Lit. Gaz.*

AN ACCOUNT of the only known MANUSCRIPT of Shakespeare's Plays, comprising some important variations and corrections in the Merry Wives of Windsor, obtained from a Playhouse copy of that Play recently discovered. By JAMES ORCHARD HALLIWELL, F.R.S. &c. 8vo, *sewed*, 1s.

THE HARROWING of HELL, a Miracle Play, written in the reign of Edward II., now first published from the Original in the British Museum, with a Modern Reading, Introduction, and Notes. By JAMES ORCHARD HALLIWELL, Esq. F.R.S. F.S.A. &c. 8vo, *sewed*, 2s.

This curious piece is supposed to be the earliest specimen of dramatic composition in the English Language: *vide* Hallam's Literature of Europe, Vol. L; Strutt's Manners and Customs, Vol. II.; Warton's English Poetry; Sharon Turner's England; Collier's History of English Dramatic Poetry, Vol. II. p. 213. *All these writers refer to the Manuscript.*

EARLY MYSTERIES; and other Latin Poems of the XIIth and XIIIth centuries. Edited from original MSS. in the British Museum, and the Libraries of Oxford, Cambridge, Paris, and Vienna. By THOS. WRIGHT, M.A., F.S.A. 8vo, bds. 4s. 6d.

ANECDOTA LITERARIA: a Collection of Short Poems in English, Latin, and French, illustrative of the Literature and History of England in the XIIIth Century; and more especially of the Condition and Manners of the different Classes of Society. By T. WRIGHT, M.A., F.S.A., &c. 8vo, *cloth*. Only 250 printed. 7s. 6d.

NUGÆ POETICÆ; Select Pieces of Old English Popular Poetry, illustrating the Manners and Arts of the XVth Century. Edited by J. O. HALLIWELL, Esq., F.R.S., &c. Post 8vo. *Only 100 copies printed, cloth*, 5s.

Contents:—Colyn Blowbol's Testament; the Debate of the Carpenter's Tools; the Merchant and his Son; the Maid and the Magpie; Elegy on Lobe, Henry VIIIth's Fool; Romance of Robert of Sicily, *and five other curious pieces of the same kind.*

TORRENT of PORTUGAL; an English Metrical Romance, *now first published*, from an unique MS. of the XVth century, preserved in the Chetham Library at Manchester. Edited by JAMES ORCHARD HALLIWELL, Esq. F.R.S. F.S.A. &c. Post 8vo, *cloth, uniform with Ritson, Weber, and Ellis's publications*, 5s.

"This is a valuable and interesting addition to our list of early English metrical romances, and an indispensable companion to the collections of Ritson, Weber, and Ellis."
Literary Gazette.

"A literary curiosity, and one both welcome and serviceable to the lover of black-letter lore. Though the obsoleteness of the style may occasion sad stumbling to a modern reader, yet the class to which it rightly belongs will value it accordingly; both because it is curious in its details, and possesses philological importance. To the general reader it presents one feature of interest, viz. the reference to Wayland Smith, whom Sir W. Scott has invested with so much interest."—*Metropolitan Magazine.*

THE MERRY TALES of the WISE MEN of GOTHAM. Edited by JAMES ORCHARD HALLIWELL, Esq. F.S.A. post 8vo, 1s.

These tales are supposed to have been composed in the early part of the sixteenth century by Dr. Andrew Borde, the well-known progenitor of Merry Andrews. "In the time of Henry the Eighth, and after," says Ant.-à-Wood, "it was accounted a book full of wit and mirth by scholars and gentlemen."

THE NOBLE and RENOWNED HISTORY of GUY, EARL of WARWICK, containing a full and true account of his many famous and valiant actions. 12mo, *new edition*, with woodcuts, *cloth*, 2s. 6d.

BY J. R. SMITH, 4, OLD COMPTON ST. SOHO.

Topographical Literature.

HISTORY and ANTIQUITIES of the HUNDRED of COMPTON, BERKS, with Dissertations on the Roman Station of Calleva Attrebatum, and the Battle of Ashdown. By W. HEWETT, Jun. 8vo. 18 *plates, cloth. Only 250 printed.* 15s.

HISTORY and ANTIQUITIES of DARTFORD, in KENT, with Incidental Notices of Places in its Neighbourhood. By J. DUNKIN, Author of the "History of the Hundreds of Bullington and Ploughley in Oxfordshire;" "History of Bicester;" "History of Bromley," &c. 8vo. 17 *plates, cloth. Only 250 printed.* 1l. 1s.

Published Monthly in royal 8vo, averaging 52 pp. and profusely illustrated with woodcuts, price 1s. per part,

THE LOCAL HISTORIAN'S TABLE BOOK of Remarkable Occurrences, Historical Facts, Traditions, Legendary and Descriptive Ballads, &c. &c., connected with the Counties of NEWCASTLE-ON-TYNE, NORTHUMBERLAND and DURHAM. By M. A. RICHARDSON. Parts I. to L. have already appeared

Volumes I, II, and III, of the "HISTORICAL DIVISION," containing 1309 pp. and 554 woodcuts may now be had in cloth, price 9s. each.
Volume I, of the "LEGENDARY DIVISION," containing 424 pp. and 31 woodcuts, cloth, 9s.

This will be found a very interesting volume to those who feel no interest in the Historical portion.

" This chronology of local occurrences, from the earliest times when a date is acertainable, possesses an especial interest for the residents of the Northern Counties; but, inasmuch as it records historical events as well as trivial incidents and biographical notices of men whose fame extended beyond their birth-places, it is not without a value to the general reader. The work is divided into two portions, the larger consisting of the chronicle, and the lesser of the traditions and ballads of the country. Some of these are very characteristic and curious; they invest with poetic associations almost every ruin or plot of ground; and the earlier legends of moss-troopers and border-strifes afford an insight into the customs and state of society in remote periods. The handsome pages are illustrated with woodcuts of old buildings and other antiquities."—*Spectator.*

" We cordially recommend this work to our friends. We are at a loss to conceive how, at so low a price, the proprietor is to be remunerated for the immense outlay incurred in its production."—*Newcastle Journal.*

NEWCASTLE TRACTS; Reprints of Rare and Curious Tracts, chiefly illustrative of the History of the Northern Counties; *beautifully printed in crown 8vo, on a fine thick paper, with Fac-simile Titles, and other features characteristic of the originals.* Only 100 copies printed. 18 Nos. sewed, 1l. 14s. 6d.
Purchasers are expected to take the succeeding Tracts as published.

HISTORIC SITES and other Remarkable and Interesting Places in the County of Suffolk. By JOHN WODDERSPOON, with Prefatory Verses by BERNARD BARTON, esq., and a Poetical Epilogue by a "SUFFOLK VILLAGER." Improved edition, *fine woodcuts,* post 8vo, pp. 232, *closely printed, and containing as much matter a many 12s. volumes,* cloth, 6s. 6d.

Principal Contents:—Framlingham Castle; Staningfield; Rookwood; Mrs. Inchbald; Aldham Common; the Martyr's Stone; Westhorpe Hall, the residence of Charles Brandon, Duke of Suffolk; Ipswich; Wolsey's Gate and Mr. Sparrow's House; Rendlesham; Redgrave; Bury St. Edmunds, the Abbey; David Hartley; Bp. Gardiner; George Bloomfield; Wetheringset; Haughley Castle; Grimstone Hall; Cavendish, the Voyager; Framlinghâm Church, the burial place of Surrey, the Poet; Bungay Castle; Dunwich; Aldborough; Wingfield, and the Old Halls of Suffolk.

A NEW GUIDE to IPSWICH, containing Notices of its Ancient and Modern History, Buildings, and Social and Commercial Condition. By JOHN WODDERSPOON. Foolscap 8vo, *fine woodcuts,* cloth, 2s. 6d.

" It is handsomely got up, and reflects great credit on Ipswich typography."—*Spectator.*

BIBLIOTHECA CANTIANA, a Bibliographical Account of what has been published on the History, Topography, Antiquities, Customs, and Family Genealogy of the COUNTY of KENT, with Biographical Notes. By JOHN RUSSELL SMITH. In a handsome 8vo volume, pp. 370, *with two plates of fac-similes of Autographs of 33 eminent Kentish Writers.* 14s. reduced to 5s.—*large paper*, 10s. 6d.

Contents—I. Historians of the County. II. Principal Maps of the County. III. Heraldic Visitations, with reference to the MSS. in the British Museum and other places. IV. Tracts printed during the Civil War and Commonwealth, 1640-1660. V. A Chronological List of all the LOCAL, PERSONAL, and PRIVATE ACTS of Parliament, (upwards of 600) which have been passed on the County, from Edward I. to Queen Victoria. VI. Works relative to the County in general. VII. Particular Parishes, Seats, Customs, and Family Genealogy, in alphabetical order. The work also comprises a notice of every Paper which has been written on the County, and published in the *Philosophical Transactions of the Royal Society, Gentleman's Magazine, Archæologia, Vetusta Monumenta, Topographer, Antiquarian Repertory,* and numerous other valuable publications, with a copious Index of every person and place mentioned throughout the volume.

" The industrious compiler of the volume before us has shown how largely the history and antiquities of Kent have already occupied the attention of Topographers and Antiquarians; and, by exhibiting in one view what is now before the public, he has at once facilitated the researches of future writers, and has pointed out how ample a field still remains for their labours. The volume contains a complete catalogue of all the printed works relative to the county, including, with respect to the most important, not only their titles in length, but also useful particulars which serve as the guide for *collation,* in ascertaining whether a book is perfect, or the principal divisions of the contents, the number of pages, lists of plates, &c. We must also mention that it is rendered more readable and interesting by the insertion of memoirs of the Kentish authors, and the plates of their autographs."—*Gentleman's Magazine.*

HISTORY of PORTSMOUTH, PORTSEA, LANDPORT, SOUTH-SEA and GOSPORT. By HENRY SLIGHT, Esq. 8vo, third Edition, *bds.* 4s.

THE VISITOR'S GUIDE to KNOLE HOUSE, near Seven Oaks in Kent, with Catalogue of the Pictures contained in the Mansion, a Genealogical History of the Sackville Family, &c. &c. By J. H. BRADY, F.R.A.S. 12mo, 27 *woodcuts by Bonner, Sly, &c. cloth,* 4s. 6d. LARGE PAPER, 10s.

" A very interesting guide to one of the most remarkable old family mansions, or we might even say, palaces, of England. The biographical notices of the portraits are very curious, and the descriptions of old trees, and other particulars in the park and gardens will amuse the gardener; while the architect will be instructed by the engravings of different parts of the house, and of the ancient furniture, more particularly of the fire-places, fire-dogs, chairs, tripods, masks, sconces, &c."—J. C. LOUDON, *Gardener's Magazine,* Jan. 1840.

ILLUSTRATIONS of KNOLE HOUSE, from Drawings by Knight, engraved on Wood by Bonner, Sly, &c. 8vo, 16 *plates with descriptions,* 5s.

GREENWICH: its History, Antiquities, and Public Buildings. By H. S. RICHARDSON. 12mo, *fine woodcuts by Baxter,* 1s. 6d.

THE FOLKESTONE FIERY SERPENT, together with the Humours of the DOVOR MAYOR; being an Ancient Ballad full of Mystery and pleasant Conceit, now first collected and printed from the various MS. copies in the possession of the inhabitants of the South-east coast of Kent, with Notes. 12mo, 1s.

THE KENTISH CORONAL, consisting of Contributions in Prose and Verse. By Writers of the County of Kent. Fcp. 8vo, pp. 192, *with frontispiece, cloth, gilt leaves,* 2s. 6d.

Among the papers inserted may be mentioned a series on the " Vegetable Productions of Kent," by ANN PRATT, author of " Flowers and their Associations;" on the Geology of Maidstone and its neighbourhood, by W. H. BENSTED; on the Historical and Traditionary Incidents connected with the County, by the Editor G. H. ADAMS, and other matters LOCALLY interesting.

A JOURNEY to BERESFORD HALL, in Derbyshire, the Seat of CHARLES COTTON, Esq. the celebrated Author and Angler. By W. ALEXANDER, F.S.A., F.L.S., late Keeper of the Prints in the British Museum. Crown 4to, *printed on tinted paper, with a spirited frontispiece, representing Walton and his adopted Son Cotton in the Fishing-house, and vignette title-page, cloth,* 5s.

Dedicated to the Anglers of Great Britain and the various Walton and Cotton Clubs. Only 100 printed.

THE ARCHÆOLOGIST and JOURNAL of ANTIQUARIAN SCIENCE, Edited by J. O. HALLIWELL, Esq. 8vo, Nos I. to X. COMPLETE, with Index, pp. 490, *with 19 engravings, cloth, reduced from* 10s. 6d. to 5s. 6d.

Containing original articles on Architecture, Historical Literature, Round Towers of Ireland, Philology, Bibliography, Topography, Proceedings of the various Antiquarian Societies, Retrospective Reviews, and Reviews of Recent Antiquarian Works, &c.

COINS of the ROMANS relating to BRITAIN, described and illustrated. By JOHN YONGE AKERMAN, F.S.A., Secretary to to the Numismatic Society, &c. Second Edition, greatly enlarged. 8vo, *with plates and woodcuts, cloth,* 10s. 6d.

ANCIENT COINS of CITIES and PRINCES, Geographically arranged and described. By J. Y. AKERMAN, F.S.A. Nos. I, II, and III.—HISPANIA, 8vo, *with* 12 *plates.* 2s. 6d. *each.*

" This promises to be a large and laborious work, but for which neither the industry nor the talents of the now long experienced author are likely to prove deficient. He has commenced with the coins of a country presenting, probably, greater room for novelty of illustration than any other, in consequence of having baffled, in a great degree, the learning and research of the most eminent numismatists."—*Gent.'s Mag.*

THE NEW TESTAMENT of our LORD and SAVIOUR JESUS CHRIST. The Text from the authorized Version, with Notes and Numismatic Illustrations, from Ancient Coins in various Public and Private Collections. By J. Y. AKERMAN, No. I. 8vo, 2s. 6d.—(*To be completed in 8 parts.*)

" Mr. Akerman's Numismatic Illustrations are not confined to the explanation of the direct allusions to different kinds of money in the sacred text; but he brings his numismatic knowledge not only to explain historical difficulties, but to furnish new and most decisive evidence of the authenticity of Holy Writ. In fact, he has done as much (if not more) for the New Testament as the Gronovii and Grævii of former days did in this department of criticism for the classical writers of antiquity. His notes are entirely explanatory, and he has carefully avoided entering into all subjects of a controversial or doctrinal nature, so that we can safely recommend his edition of the New Testament to all classes of readers, to whatever religious sect they may belong.
Literary Gazette.

NUMISMATIC CHRONICLE and PROCEEDINGS of the NUMISMATIC SOCIETY, 5 vols. and 3 Nos. to Oct. 1843; *a subscriber's copy, many plates, cloth,* 2l. 12s. 6d. (pub. at 3l. 17s.)

Heraldry and Genealogy.

THE CURIOSITIES OF HERALDRY, with Illustrations from old English Writers. By MARK ANTONY LOWER, Author of " Essays on English Surnames;" *with Illuminated Title-page, and numerous Engravings from designs by the Author.* 8vo, *cloth,* GULES, *appropriately ornamented,* OR. 14s.

Contents :—Chap. I. The Fabulous History of Heraldry. II. The Authentic History of Heraldry. III. Rationale of Heraldric Charges. IV. The Chimerical Figures of Heraldry. V. The Language of Arms. VI. Allusive Arms. VII. Observations on Crests, Supporters, Badges, &c. VIII. Mottoes. IX. Anecdotes relative to the acquisition of arms and Augmentations ; X. Desultory Remarks on Titles of Honour. XI. Brief Historical Sketch of the College of Arms. XII. Notices of Heraldric Authors and their Works, from the 15th century to the 19th. XIII. Genealogy.—Appendix. On the Differences of Arms, by Sir Edw. Dering, Bart., *now first printed.* Exemplifications of the Practice of Deriving Arms from those of feudal superiors, &c. drawn from the County of Cornwall, and several other curious Papers.

A GENEALOGICAL and HERALDIC HISTORY of the EXTINCT and DORMANT BARONETCIES of England, Ireland, and Scotland. By J. BURKE, Esq. and J. B. BURKE, Esq. Medium 8vo, SECOND EDITION. 638 *closely printed pages, in double columns, with about* 1000 *arms engraved on wood, fine portrait of* JAMES I, *and illuminated title-page,* extra cloth, 10s., published at 1l. 8s.

This work, which has engaged the attention of the Authors for several years, comprises nearly a thousand families, many of them amongst the most ancient and eminent in the kingdom, each carried down to its representative or representatives still existing, with elaborate and minute details of the alliances, achievements, and fortunes, generation after generation, from the earliest to the latest period. The work is printed to correspond precisely with the last edition of Mr. Burke's Dictionary of the Existing Peerage and Baronetage; the armorial bearings are engraved in the best style, and are incorporated with the text as in that work.

A GENERAL ARMORY of ENGLAND, SCOTLAND, and IRELAND; comprising a Registry of all Armorial Bearings, from the earliest to the present time. By J. BURKE, Esq. and J. B. BURKE, Esq. Royal 8vo, THIRD EDITION, with Supplement. 1200 *pages, in double columns, illuminated title-page,* cloth, 1l. 1s. published at 2l. 2s.

The most useful book on Heraldry extant; it embodies all the arms of Guillim, Edmonson, Robson, Berry and others, prefaced by a history of the art.

Provincial Dialects of England.

POEMS of RURAL LIFE, in the DORSET DIALECT, with a Dissertation and Glossary. By WILLIAM BARNES, royal 12mo, cloth, 10s.

A GLOSSARY of PROVINCIAL WORDS and PHRASES in use in Wiltshire, shewing their Derivation in numerous instances from the Language of the Anglo-Saxons. By JOHN YONGE AKERMAN, Esq. F.S.A. 12mo, *cloth,* 3s.

WESTMORLAND and CUMBERLAND DIALECTS. Dialogues, Poems, Songs, and Ballads, by various Writers, in the Westmorland and Cumberland Dialects, now first collected, to which is added, a Copious Glossary of Words peculiar to those Counties. Post 8vo, pp. 408, *cloth,* 9s.

This collection comprises, in the *Westmorland Dialect,* Mrs. ANN WHEELER'S Four Familiar Dialogues, with Poems, &c.; and in the *Cumberland Dialect*, I. Poems and Pastorals by the Rev. JOSIAH RELPH; II. Pastorals, &c., by EWAN CLARK; III. Letter from Dublin by a young Borrowdale Shepherd, by ISAAC RITSON; IV. Poems by JOHN STAGG; V. Poems by MARK LONSDALE; VI. Ballads and Songs by ROBERT ANDERSON, the Cumbrian Bard (*including some now first printed*); VII. Songs by Miss BLAMIRE and Miss GILPIN; VIII. Songs by JOHN RAYSON; IX. An Extensive Glossary of Westmorland and Cumberland Words.

> " Among the specimens of Cumberland Verse will be found some true poetry, if not the best ever written in the language of rural life this side the Scotch Borders. The writers seem to have caught in their happiest hours inspiration from the rapt soul of Burns. Anderson's touching song of wedded love, ' The Days that are geane,' is a worthy answer for a husband to Burn's ' John Anderson my Jo.' " —*Gent's. Magazine.*

> " No other two counties in England have so many pieces, both in prose and verse, illustrative of the manners and customs of the inhabitants, and written in their own native dialect. The philologist will find numerous examples of words and phrases which are obsolete in the general language of England, or which have been peculiar to Westmorland and Cumberland from time immemorial. Nor are the pieces uninteresting in other respects. Some of the *patois* verses are rich in the true spirit and vigour of poetry."—*Metropolitan.*

> " A charming volume: it contains some beautiful poetical effusions, as well as characteristic sketches in prose."—*Archæologist.*

THE VOCABULARY of EAST ANGLIA, an attempt to record the vulgar tongue of the twin sister Counties, *Norfolk* and *Suffolk*, as it existed in the last twenty years of the Eighteenth Century, and still exists; with proof of its Antiquity from Etymology and Authority. By the Rev. R. FORBY. 2 vols. post 8vo, *cloth,* 12s. (original price 1l. 1s.)

GROSE'S (FRANCIS, F.S.A.) GLOSSARY of PROVINCIAL and LOCAL WORDS used in ENGLAND, with which is now first incorporated the SUPPLEMENT by SAMUEL PEGGE, F.S.A. Post 8vo, *elegantly printed, cloth*, 4s. 6d.

The utility of a Provincial Glossary to all persons desirous of understanding our ancient poets is so universally acknowledged, that to enter into a proof of it would be entirely a work of supererogation. Grose and Pegge are constantly referred to in Todd's "Johnson's Dictionary."

EXMOOR SCOLDING and COURTSHIP in the Propriety and Decency of Exmoor (Devonshire) Language, *with Notes and a Glossary*. Post 8vo, 12th edition, 1s. 6d.

"A very rich bit of West of Englandism."—*Metropolitan*.

OBSERVATIONS on some of the DIALECTS of the WEST of ENGLAND, particularly *Somersetshire*, with a Glossary of Words now in use there, and Poems and other Pieces, exemplifying the Dialect. By JAMES JENNINGS. 12mo, pp. 210, 3s.

A COLLECTION of FUGITIVE PIECES in the DIALECT of ZUMMERZET. Edited by J. O. HALLIWELL. Post 8vo, *only 50 printed*, 2s.

A GLOSSARY of some Words used in CHESHIRE, by ROGER WILBRAHAM, Esq., F.R.S. and S.A. 12mo, 2d edition, *with additions*, 3s.

THE YORKSHIRE DIALECT, exemplified in various Dialogues, Tales, and Songs, applicable to the County, with a Glossary. Post 8vo, 1s.

"A shilling book worth its money: most of the pieces of composition are not only harmless, but good and pretty. The eclogue on the death of 'Awd Daisy,' an outworn horse, is an outpouring of some of the best feelings of the rustic mind; and the addresses to riches and poverty have much of the freedom and spirit of Burns."

Gent's Magazine, May 1841.

THE HALLAMSHIRE (district of Sheffield) GLOSSARY, by the Rev. JOSEPH HUNTER. Post 8vo, *bds*. 5s.

It also contains Thoresby's Catalogue of Yorkshire Words, and Watson's uncommon words used in Halifax.

THE BAIRNSLA FOAKS' ANNUAL, an onny body els as beside for't years 1842 and 1843. Be TOM TREDDLEHOYLE. To which is added the Barnsley and Village Record, or the Book of Facts and Fancies. By NED NUT. 12mo, pp. 100, 1s.

This almanac is written in the Barnsley Dialect, and therefore fits itself with peculiar emphasis to the understanding of all in that particular locality. Its influence, however, extends beyond this; for even those unacquainted with the Barnsley peculiarities of speech, will find much amusement in perusing the witticisms of the author, through his curious mode of expression.

SHEFFIELD DIALECT; with a Glossary, and general Rules for understanding the Orthography. By ABEL BYWATER. 12mo, cloth, 3s. 6d.

THE NEWCASTLE SONG BOOK, or Tyne-Side Songster, being a Collection of Comic and Satirical Songs, descriptive of Eccentric Characters, and the Manners and Customs of a portion of the labouring population of *Newcastle-on-Tyne*, and the Neighbourhood, *chiefly in the Newcastle Dialect*. 12mo, 4 parts complete, 1s. each.

LANCASHIRE DIALECT, or TUMMUS and MEARY, being the Laughable Adventures of a Lancashire Clown. By TIM BOBBIN. 12mo, 1s.

DICK and SAL, or JACK and JOAN'S FAIR, a Doggerel Poem, in the Kentish Dialect. 3d edition, 12mo, 6d.

§

10 VALUABLE AND INTERESTING BOOKS ON SALE

TOM CLADPOLE'S JOURNEY to LUNNUN, told by himself, and written in pure SUSSEX Doggerel, by his Uncle Tim. 18mo, 5th thousand, 6d.

JAN CLADPOLE'S TRIP to 'MERRICUR in Search for Dollar Trees, and how he got rich enough to beg his way home! written in Sussex Doggerel. 12mo, 6d.

JOHN NOAKES and MARY STYLES, a Poem, *exhibiting some of the most striking lingual localisms peculiar to Essex*, with a Glossary. By CHARLES CLARK, Esq. of Great Totham Hall, Essex. Post 8vo, cloth, 2s.

"The poem possesses considerable humour." *Tait's Mag.*—"A very pleasant trifle." *Lit. Gaz.*—"A very clever production." *Essex Lit. Journal.*—"Full of rich humour." *Essex Mercury.*—"Very droll." *Metropolitan.*—"Exhibits the dialect of Essex perfectly." *Eclectic Review.*—"Full of quaint wit and humour." *Gent's Mag. May* 1841. —"A very clever and amusing piece of local description." *Archæologist.*

BOUCHER'S GLOSSARY of ARCHAIC and PROVINCIAL WORDS. Edited by Hunter and Stevenson. Parts I & II. (*all published*) 9s. (pub. at 18s.)

BIBLIOGRAPHICAL LIST of all the Works which have been published towards illustrating the Provincial Dialects of England. By JOHN RUSSELL SMITH. Post 8vo, 1s.

"Very serviceable to such as prosecute the study of our provincial dialects, or are collecting works on that curious subject. We very cordially recommend it to notice."
Metropolitan.

HISTOIRE LITTERAIRE, PHILOLOGIQUE et BIBLIOGRA- PHIQUE des PATOIS. Par PIERQUIN de GEMBLOUX. 8vo, Paris, 1841. 8s. 6d.

THE ANGLO-SAXON VERSION of the HOLY GOSPELS. Edited by B. THORPE. Post 8vo, cloth, 9s. 6d.

AN INTRODUCTION to ANGLO-SAXON READING; comprising, Ælfric's Homily on the Birthday of St. Gregory, with a copious Glossary, &c. By L. LANGLEY, F.L.S. 12mo, *cloth*, 2s. 6d.

THE EARLY HISTORY of FREEMASONRY in ENGLAND, Illustrated by an English Poem of the XIVth Century, with Notes. By J. O. HALLIWELL, F.S.A. Post 8vo, Second Edition, *with a fac-simile of the original MS. in the British Museum.* 2s. 6d.

"The interest which the curious poem of which this publication is chiefly composed has excited, is proved by the fact of its having been translated into German, and of its having reached a second edition, which is not common with such publications. Mr. Halliwell has carefully revised the new edition, and increased its utility by the addition of a complete and correct glossary."—*Literary Gazette.*

GENOA: with Remarks on the Climate, and its Influence upon Invalids. By HENRY JONES BUNNETT, M.D. 12mo, cloth, 4s.

A PLAIN and FAMILIAR EXPLICATION of CHRIST'S PRE- SENCE in the SACRAMENT out of the Doctrine of the Church of England, for 'the satisfying of a Scrupulous Friend,' Anno 1631. By that incomparable Prelate, JOSEPH HALL, D.D., formerly Lord Bishop of Norwich. Post 8vo, *beautifully printed with various coloured inks, a curious specimen of typography,* cloth, 2s. 6d.

Witchcraft and Delusion.

TRIAL of the WITCHES at BURY ST. EDMUNDS, before Sir M. HALE, 1664, with an Appendix, by CHARLES CLARK, Esq. of Totham, Essex. 8vo, 1s.

"The most perfect Narrative of anything of this nature hitherto extant."—*Preface.*

WONDERFUL DISCOVERY of the WITCHCRAFTS of MARGARET and PHILIP FLOWER, daughters of Joan Flower, near Bever (Belvoir), executed at LINCOLN for confessing themselves actors in the destruction of Lord Rosse, son of the Earl of Rutland, 1618. 8vo, 1s.

One of the most extraordinary cases of Witchcraft on record.

ACCOUNT of the TRIAL, CONFESSION, and CONDEMNATION of SIX WITCHES at MAIDSTONE, 1652; also the Trial and Execution of three others at Faversham, 1645. 8vo, 1s.

These transactions are unnoticed by all the Kentish historians.

A FAITHFUL RECORD of the MIRACULOUS CASE of MARY JOBSON. By W. REID CLANNY, M.D. of Sunderland. 8vo, 1s. 6d.

The second edition of a most extraordinary Narrative, which has caused great sensation in the North of England.

Publications of James Orchard Halliwell.

RARA MATHEMATICA; or a Collection of Treatises on the Mathematics and Subjects connected with them, from ancient inedited MSS. 8vo, Second Edition, *cloth*, 3s. 6d.

Contents: Johannis de Sacro-Bosco Tractatus de Arte Numerandi; Method used in England in the Fifteenth Century for taking the Altitude of a Steeple; Treatise on the Numeration of Algorism; Treatise on Glasses for Optical Purposes, by W. Bourne; Johannis Robyns de Cometis Commentaria; Two Tables showing the time of High Water at London Bridge, and the Duration of Moonlight, from a MS. of the Thirteenth Century; on the Mensuration of Heights and Distances; Alexandri de Villa Dei Carmen de Algorismo; Preface to a Calendar or Almanack for 1430; Johannis Norfolk in Artem progressionis summula; Notes on Early Almanacs, by the Editor, &c. &c.

MANUSCRIPT RARITIES of the UNIVERSITY of CAMBRIDGE. 8vo, *boards*, 6s.

A companion to Hartshorne's "Book Rarities" of the same University.

ON the CHARACTER of SIR JOHN FALSTAFF, as originally exhibited by Shakspeare in the Two Parts of King Henry IV. 12mo, *cloth*, (*very few printed*,) 4s. 6d.

RELIQUÆ ANTIQUÆ. Scraps from Ancient Manuscripts, illustrating chiefly Early English Literature and the English Language. Edited by WRIGHT and HALLIWELL. 2 vols. 8vo, *complete, half morocco, uncut,* 2l.

ACCOUNT of the LIFE, WRITINGS, and INVENTIONS of Sir SAMUEL MORLAND, Master of Mechanics to Charles II. 8vo, 1s.

JOHANNIS DE SACRO-BOSCO, *Anglici,* DE ARTE NUMERANDI TRACTATUS. 8vo, 1s.

TWO ESSAYS: I. On the Bœotian Numerical Contractions II. Notes on Early Almanacs. 8vo, 1s.

A FEW HINTS to NOVICES in MANUSCRIPT LITERATURE. 8vo, 1s.

A CATALOGUE of the CONTENTS of the CODEX HOLBROOKIANUS. 8vo, 1s.

THE CONNEXION of WALES with the EARLY SCIENCE of ENGLAND. 8vo, 1s.

HISTORIA COLLEGII JESU CANTABRIGIENSIS à J. SHERMANNO, olim præs. ejusdem Collegii. 8vo, (*Cambridge Antiquarian Society*,) 2s.

A FEW NOTES on the HISTORY of the DISCOVERY of the COMPOSITION of WATER. 8vo, 1s.

CATALOGUE of the MISCELLANEOUS MANUSCRIPTS preserved in the Library of the Royal Society. 8vo, 2s.

MANAGEMENT of COVENT GARDEN THEATRE vindicated from the Attack of an Anonymous Critic, in a Letter to the Editor of the "Cambridge Advertiser." 8vo, (not printed for sale,) 1s.

AN ACCOUNT of the EUROPEAN MANUSCRIPTS in the CHETHAM LIBRARY, MANCHESTER. 12mo, 1s.

OBSERVATIONS upon the HISTORY of CERTAIN EVENTS in ENGLAND, temp. Edward IV. (from the Archæologia) 4to, 1s. 6d.

OBSERVATIONS on the CONTENTS of the "SPECULUM CHRISTIANA," (a work of the Lollards,) and on its real Author, (from the Archæologia,) 4to, 6d.

ON the VOLVELLE and on CHAUCER'S TREATISE on the ASTROLABE, (from the Archæologia,) 4to, 6d.

PORTRAIT of JAMES ORCHARD HALLIWELL, drawn from Life and on Stone by W. L. WALTON. 4to, proofs on India Paper, (only 100 printed,) 2s. 6d.

REPORT EXTRAORDINARY of a late Meeting of the Society of Antiquaries, in a Letter to "PUNCH," occasioned by a remarkable Omission in that Gentleman's Account of the Metropolis. Post 8vo, 6d.

ENGLISH MONASTIC LIBRARIES. I. Catalogue of the Library of the Priory of Bretton, Yorkshire. II. Notice of the Libraries belonging to other Religious Houses. By the Rev. JOSEPH HUNTER, F.S.A. 4to, very few printed, 5s.

Publications of the Camden Society, 1838-44.

(Not printed for sale), all 4to, in cloth.

" The prices maintained by our books, when copies get abroad in the market, afford encouraging proof of the demand for them on the part of collectors and literary men. In four years the Society has issued eighteen volumes, all of them works excluded from the ordinary mode of publication, and yet worthy of being published, of eminent use to historical inquirers, and likely to retain a place in the permanent literature of the country."—*Report of the Council*, 1842.

HISTORIE of the ARRIVAL of EDWARD IV. in ENGLAND, and the finall recoverye of his Kingdomes from Henry VI. 1471. Edited by BRUCE. 10s. 6d.

KYNG JOHAN, a PLAY, by JOHN BALE, (now first printed.) Edited by J. P. COLLIER. 7s. 6d.

ALLITERATIVE POEM on the DEPOSITION of KING RICH. II. with a Glossary—Ric. Maydestone de Concordia inter. Rich. II. et Civitatem, London. Edited by WRIGHT. 10s. 6d.

PLUMPTON CORRESPONDENCE; a Series of Letters written in the reigns of Edward IV. to Henry VIII. by the Plumpton Family of Yorkshire. Edited by STAPLETON. pp. 450, 1l. 1s.

ANECDOTES and TRADITIONS, illustrative of Early English History and Literature, derived from MS. sources. Edited by THOMS. 15s.

POLITICAL SONGS of ENGLAND, from the reign of John to
that of Edward II. Edited and translated by WRIGHT. pp. 426. 10s. 6d.

ANNALS of the FIRST FOUR YEARS of the Reign of QUEEN
ELIZABETH. By Sir JOHN HAYWARD, *now first printed;* and edited by BRUCE. 6s.

ECCLESIASTICAL DOCUMENTS, viz. 1. A Brief History of the
Bishoprick of Somerset to the year 1174. 2. Curious Collection of Charters from the Library of Dr. Cox Macro. *Now first published.* By Rev JOSEPH HUNTER. 4s. 6d.

HISTORICAL and CHOROGRAPHICAL DESCRIPTION of the
COUNTY of ESSEX. By JOHN NORDEN, 1594. *Now first printed,* and edited by Sir H. ELLIS. VERY CURIOUS MAP, 6s.

CHRONICLE of the FIRST THIRTEEN YEARS of the Reign
of Edward IV. By JOHN WARKWORTH. *Now first printed,* and edited by HALLIWELL. 4s. 6d.

KEMP'S NINE DAIES WONDER, performed in a Daunce from
London to Norwich, with Introduction and Notes by DYCE. 5s.

"A great curiosity, and, as a rude picture of national manners, extremely well worth reprinting."—*Gifford's Notes to Ben Jonson.*

EGERTON PAPERS. A Collection of Public and Private Documents, chiefly illustrative of the Times of Elizabeth and James I. from the original MSS. the property of Lord Francis Egerton. Edited by J. P. COLLIER, pp. 518. 14s.

"Mr. Collier has fallen into a rich field, and full of pasture, among the Egerton papers. They seem to be stored with abundant materials, and the single volume before us is a valuable sample of their national interest, and which throw a light upon public events hitherto imperfectly appreciated."—*Lit. Gaz.*

CHRONICA JOCELINA de BRAKELONDA, de Rebus Gestis
Samsonis Abbatis Monasterii Sancti Edmundi: nunc primum typis mandata curante J. GAGE-ROKEWODE. 10s. 6d.

"There is one publication which the Society may well be gratified at having been the means of adding to the materials of the History of England, the Chronicle of Josceline de Brakelond, a work edited with singular care and judgment, and unique in its character, as affording an illustration of monastic life more vivid and complete than can be found in any work with which the Council are acquainted."

Report of the C. S. 1841.

NARRATIVES illustrative of the CONTESTS in IRELAND in
1641 and 1693. Edited by T. C. CROKER. 6s.

CHRONICLE of WILLIAM of RISHANGER of the Barons'
Wars—The Miracles of Simon de Montfort. Ed. from MSS. by J. O. HALLIWELL. 7s.

LATIN POEMS, commonly attributed to Walter de Mapes, Archdeacon of Oxford in the XIIIth Century. Edited by T. WRIGHT. pp. 420. 12s.

The Appendix contains some very curious translations of the poems (many now first printed), in Anglo-Norman, French, Scotch, and English, from the 13th to the 16th century.

TRAVELS of NICANDER NUCIUS of CORCYRA in ENGLAND,
during the Reign of Henry VIII. Edited by Dr. CRAMER. 6s.

THREE EARLY ENGLISH METRICAL ROMANCES (the
Anturs of Arthur at the Tarnewathelan; Sir Amadace; and the Avowing of King Arthur, Sir Gawan, Sir Kaye, and Sir Bawdewyn of Bretan), with Glossary, &c. By J. ROBSON. 7s. 6d.

PRIVATE DIARY of DR. JOHN DEE, and the Catalogue of his
Library of MSS., now first printed. Edited by J. O HALLIWELL. 6s.

" It gives the reader a most curious insight into the " sayings and doings" of this celebrated man during his residence at Mortlake in Surrey.

APOLOGY for LOLLARD DOCTRINES attributed to Wicliffe.
Now first printed, and edited by Dr. J. H TODD. pp. 269. 9s.

RUTLAND PAPERS. Documents relating to the Coronation of Henry VII. the Field of the Cloth of Gold, and the interviews of Henry VIII. with the Emperor. From the Duke of Rutland's MS. collections. Edited by W. JERDAN. 8s.

DIARY of DR. THOMAS CARTWRIGHT, Bishop of Chester, Aug. 1686 to Oct. 1687, now first printed. Ed. by the Rev JOSEPH HUNTER. 6s. 6d.

Cartwright was one of James the Second's creatures for the purpose of furthering Popery in England, and also principal commissioner for depriving Dr. Hough of the Presidency of Magdalen College, Oxford.

ORIGINAL LETTERS of EMINENT LITERARY MEN of the XVIth, XVIIth, and XVIIIth Centuries, from the originals in the British Museum and the Bodleian Library, with Notes by Sir HENRY ELLIS. pp. 468, *facsimiles*, 10s.

" The Council anticipate that when generally known this volume will be one of the most highly esteemed among the publications of the Society. It preserves many particulars relating to Camden and his great work the Britannia; others respecting the formation and early application to the purposes of literature of the invaluable collection of MSS. formed by Sir Robert Cotton; and is, in truth, a collection of interesting memorials of the literature of the last three centuries."—*Report of the Council*, 1843.

A CONTEMPORARY NARRATIVE of the proceedings against DAME ALLICE KYTLER, prosecuted for SORCERY in 1324. By RICHARD de LEDREDE, Bishop of Ossory. Edited by THOMAS WRIGHT. 5s.

This volume affords a curious picture of the turbulent state of Ireland in the Reign of Edward II. and an interesting chapter in the history of English Superstition.

PROMPTORIUM Parvulorum sive Clericorum, Lexicon Anglo-Latinum princeps, autore Fratre Galfrido Grammatico Dicto e Predicationibus Lenne Episcopi Northfolciensi A.D. 1440, olim e prelis Pynsonianis editum, nunc ab integro, commentariolis subjectis, ad fidem codicum recensuit ALBERTUS WAY. Tomus prior, 10s. 6d.

A COLLECTION of ORIGINAL LETTERS relating to the DISSOLUTION of the MONASTERIES, and some other points connected with the Reformation. Edited by THOMAS WRIGHT. 10s. 6d.

LETTERS and STATE PAPERS relating to the Proceedings of the Earl of Leicester in the Low Countries, 1585-6. Edited by BRUCE. pp. 500, 14s.

A FRENCH CHRONICLE of LONDON, from the 44th of Henry III to the 17th of Edw. III, *with copious English notes*. By J. G. AUNGIER. 6s.

POLYDORE VERGIL'S History of the Reigns of Henry VI, Edward IV, and Richard III, *now first printed in English from a MS. in the British Museum*. By Sir H. ELLIS. 7s. 6d.

THE THORNTON ROMANCES. The Early English Metrical Romances of Perceval, Isumbras, Eglamour, and Degrevant, selected from MSS. at Lincoln and Cambridge. By J. O. HALLIWELL. 12s.

N.B. The above 30 volumes are all the Society have published; complete sets will be sold for £10 10s., the succeeding ones will be on sale as they appear.

Publications of the Percy Society, 1840-44.

Elegantly printed in post 8vo, (not printed for Sale.)

OLD BALLADS of the utmost rarity, now first collected and edited by J. P. COLLIER. 4s. 6d.

ROWLEY'S SEARCH for MONEY, reprinted from the Edition of 1609. 2s.

PAIN and SORROW of EVIL MARRIAGE, from an unique copy, printed by WYNKYN DE WORDE. 2s. 6d.

A SELECTION from the Minor Poems of DAN JOHN LYDGATE. Edited by HALLIWELL. pp. 284. 9s.

THE KING and a POOR NORTHERN MAN, from the Edition of 1640. 1s. 6d.
The old story of the Farmer's going to Windsor to see the King about a flaw in the lease of his farm.

HISTORICAL SONGS of IRELAND, illustrative of the Struggle between James II. and William III. with Introduction and Notes, by T. C. CROKER. 4s.

COLLECTION of SONGS and BALLADS, relative to the London 'Prentices and Trades, and London generally. Edited by C. MACKAY. 5s.

EARLY NAVAL BALLADS of ENGLAND, collected and Edited by J. O. HALLIWELL. 4s.

ROBIN GOODFELLOW; his Mad Pranks and Merry Jests, full of honest mirth. 2s.

STRANGE HISTORIES, consisting of Ballads and other Poems, principally by THOMAS DELONEY, 1607. 4s.

POLITICAL BALLADS, published in England during the Commonwealth. Edited by THOMAS WRIGHT. pp. 300, 6s.

PLEASANT HISTORY of the TWO ANGRY WOMEN of ABINGDON, with the Humorous Mirth of Dick Coomes and Nicholas Proverbs. A Play by HENRY PORTER, 1599. Edited by the Rev. A. DYCE. 4s.

THE BOKE of CURTASYE, an English Poem of the XVth Century. Edited by J. O. HALLIWELL. 2s. 6d.

MEETING of GALLANTS at an ORDINARIE, or the WALKES in POWLES. Edited by HALLIWELL. 3s.

KIND-HEART'S DREAM, by HENRY CHETTLE. Edited by E. F. RIMBAULT. 4s.

SPECIMENS of OLD CHRISTMAS CAROLS. Edited by WRIGHT. 3s.

NURSERY RHYMES of ENGLAND, collected principally from Oral Tradition. By HALLIWELL. 6s.
Of this a third and enlarged edition is now ready, *see page 2 of this list.*

HISTORY of PATIENT GRISEL, with Introduction, 3s.

SPECIMENS of LYRIC POETRY, of the Reign of Edward I. Edited by WRIGHT. 4s. 6d.

MARRIAGE TRIUMPH on the NUPTIALS of the PRINCE PALATINE and the PRINCESS ELIZABETH, daughter of James I. by THOMAS HEYWOOD. Edited by COLLIER. 2s. 6d.

A KNIGHT'S CONJURING done in EARNEST, discovered in JEST, by THOMAS DEKKER, Edited by RIMBAULT. 3s. 6d.

A PARAPHRASE on the SEVEN PENITENTIAL PSALMS in ENGLISH VERSE, by THOMAS BRAMPTON, 1414, together with the Psalter of St. Bernard. Edited by W. H. BLACK. 4s. 6d.

CROWN GARLAND of ROSES, consisting of Ballads and Songs, by R. JOHNSON, 1612. Edited by W. CHAPPELL. 3s.

DIALOGUE concerning WITCHES and WITCHCRAFTS, by GEORGE GIFFORD, Vicar of Maldon, 1603. Edited by WRIGHT. 4s. 6d.

This dialogue was thought to merit reprinting, both as being an excellent specimen of the colloquial language of the reign of Elizabeth, and for the good sense with which the writer treats a subject on which so many people ran mad, and the curious allusions which it contains to the superstitions of that age.

FOLLIES' ANATOMIE, or SATYRES and SATYRICALL EPIGRAMS, by HENRY HUTTON. *Dunelmensis*, 1619. Edited by RIMBAULT. 3s.

JACK of DOVER, his Quest of Iuquirie, or his Privy Search for the veriest Foole in England, a collection of Merry Tales. 1604. 2s. 6d.

This tract is exceedingly curious, as forming one of the links between the wit of the middle ages, and that of modern times. There is scarcely one of the "merry tales" contained in it which has not its counterpart among the numerous Latin stories of the monks, which were popular in the thirteenth and fourteenth centuries.

ANCIENT POETICAL TRACTS of the XVIth Century, reprinted from unique copies. Edited by RIMBAULT. 3s. 6d.

A SELECTION of LATIN STORIES, from MSS. of the XIIIth and XIVth Centuries. Edited by WRIGHT. pp. 280, 6s.

THE HARMONY of the CHURCH, SPIRITUAL SONGS and HOLY HYMNS, by MICHAEL DRAYTON, reprinted from the Edition of 1591, (and not in his collected works.) Edited by DYCE. 3s.

COCK LORRELL'S BOTE, a Satyrical Poem, from an unique copy, printed by WYNKYN de WORDE. Edited by RIMBAULT. 2s.

POEMS by SIR HENRY WOTTON. Edited by DYCE. 1s. 6d.

THE HARMONY of BIRDS, a Poem, from the only known copy printed in the middle of the sixteenth Century, with Introduction. 2s.

A KERRY PASTORAL, in Imitation of the First Eclogue of VIRGIL. Edited with Introduction, by T. C. CROKER. *Woodcuts*, 2s.

A curious picture of Irish manners about the beginning of the eighteenth century.

THE FOUR KNAVES, a Series of Satirical Tracts. By SAMUEL ROWLANDS. 1611-13. Edited, with introduction and Notes, by RIMBAULT. Woodcuts, 4s. 6d.

A POEM to the MEMORY of WILLIAM CONGREVE, by JAMES THOMSON. Edited by P. CUNNINGHAM. 1s. 6d.

PLEASANT CONCEITES of OLD HOBSON, the Merry Londoner, full of humourous discourses and witty merriments, whereat the quickest wittes may laugh, and the wiser sort take pleasure. 1607. Edited by HALLIWELL. 2s.

MAROCCUS EXTATICUS; or, BANKES'S BAY HORSE in a TRANCE: anatomizing some abuses and bad tricks of this age (1595). Edited by RIMBAULT. 1s. 6d.

LORD MAYORS' PAGEANTS; being Collections towards a History of these annual celebrations: with specimens of the descriptive pamphlets published by the City poets. Edited by F. W. FAIRHOLT. Part I. Woodcuts, 5s.

——————————— Part II. 5s.

BY J. R. SMITH, 4, OLD COMPTON ST. SOHO. 17

OWL and the NIGHTINGALE, a Poem of the 13th Century; attributed to NICHOLAS DE GUILDFORD: with some shorter Poems from the same MSS. Edited by WRIGHT. 2s. 6d.

THIRTEEN PSALMS, and the First Chapter of Ecclesiastes, translated into English Verse by JOHN CROKE, temp. Henry VIII, with Documents relative to the Croke Family. Edited by BLISS. 2s. 6d.

HISTORICALL EXPOSTULATION against the beastlye Abusers both of Chyrurgerie and Physyke in oure Time: by JOHN HALLE, (with portrait.) Edited by PETTIGREW. 2s. 6d.

OLD BALLADS; illustrating the great Frost of 1683-4, and the Fair on the River Thames. Edited by RIMBAULT. 3s.

HONESTIE OF THIS AGE; proving by Good Circumstance that the World was never Honest till now. By BARNABY RICH, 1614. Edited by P. CUNNINGHAM. 3s.

HISTORY of REYNARD the FOX, from CAXTON's edition in 1481, with Notes and Literary History of the Romance. Edited by W. J. THOMS. 6s.

THE KEEN (FUNERAL LAMENTATIONS) of the South of Ireland, illustrative of Irish Political and Domestic History, Manners, Music, and Superstitions. Edited by T. C. CROKER, 4s.

POEMS of JOHN AUDELAY, a specimen of the Shropshire Dialect in the XVth Century. Edited by HALLIWELL. 3s. 6d.

ST. BRANDRAN; a Medieval Legend of the Sea, in English Verse and Prose. Edited by WRIGHT. 3s.

ROMANCE of the EMPEROR OCTAVIAN, now first published from MSS. at Lincoln and Cambridge, edited by HALLIWELL. 2s. 6d.

SIX BALLADS with BURDENS, from a MS. at Cambridge, edited by GOODWIN. 1s. 6d.

LYRICAL POEMS, selected from Musical Publications, 1589 and 1600. Edited by COLLIER. 3s. 6d.

FRIAR BAKON'S PROPHESIE; a Satire on the Degeneracy of the Times, A.D. 1604. Edited by HALLIWELL. 1s. 6d.

N.B.—The above 52 pieces are all the Society have published.

Publications of the Shakspeare Society, 1841-44.

(Not printed for Sale) all 8vo, in cloth.

MEMOIRS of EDWARD ALLEYN, Founder of Dulwich College, including new particulars of Shakspeare, Ben Johnson, Massinger, Marston, &c. by J. P. COLLIER. 7s. 6d.

THE SCHOOL of ABUSE, containing a Pleasant Invective against Poets, Pipers, Players, &c. by STEPHEN GOSSON, 1579—HEYWOOD'S (THOMAS) Apology for Actors, 1612, reprinted in one vol. 5s.

LUDUS COVENTRIÆ—A Collection of Mysteries formerly represented at Coventry, on the Feast of Corpus Christi. Edited, with Notes and Glossary, by J. O. HALLIWELL. A thick volume, 12s.

A DEBATE between PRIDE and LOWLINESS, by FRANCIS THYNNE. Edited by J. P. COLLIER. 8vo, 4s. 6d.

PATIENT GRISEL, A Comedy by DEKKER, CHETTLE, and HAUGHTON, with Introduction by COLLIER. 8vo, 5s.

EXTRACTS from the ACCOUNTS of the REVELS at COURT, temp. Queen Elizabeth and James I, with Introduction and Notes by P. CUNNINGHAM. 6s.

FIRST SKETCH of SHAKSPEARE'S MERRIE WIVES of WINDSOR, with a collection of the Tales on which the Plot is supposed to have been founded. Edited by HALLIWELL. 4s. 6d. 1842.

NOTES on BEN JONSON'S CONVERSATIONS with WILLIAM DRUMMOND of Hawthornden. Edited by LAING. 5s. 1842.

FOOLS and JESTERS, with a reprint of ROBERT ARMIN'S NEST of NINNIES, 1608. Edited by COLLIER. 4s. 6d. 1842.

THE OLD PLAY of TIMON of ATHENS, which preceded that of Shakspeare, *now first printed from a MS.* Edited by DYCE. 3s. 6d.

PIERCE PENNILESS'S SUPPLICATION to the DEVIL. By THOMAS NASH, 1592. With Introduction and Notes by COLLIER. 4s.

HEYWOOD'S (THOMAS) FIRST and SECOND PARTS of KING EDWARD VI, with Notes by BARRON FIELD. 4s. 6d.

NORTHBROOKE'S TREATISE against DICE, DANCING, PLAYS, and other IDLE PASTIMES, 1577. Edited by COLLIER. 4s. 6d.

OBERON'S VISION in the MIDSUMMER NIGHTS' DREAM, illustrated by a comparison with LYLIE'S Endymion. By the Rev. J. HALPIN. 4s. 6d.

THE FIRST SKETCHES of the SECOND and THIRD PARTS of KING HENRY the SIXTH. With Introduction and Notes by HALLIWELL. 5s.

The possessor of this volume will have the two Plays upon which Shakspeare founded his Second and Third Parts of Henry VI. both printed from *unique* copies in the Bodleian—one a small octavo, which cost at Chalmers's sale, £130; the other a very thin small quarto, which cost £64 several years ago, and would now probably realize more than twice that sum.

THE CHESTER PLAYS: a Collection of Mysteries founded upon Scriptural Subjects, and formerly represented by the Trades of Chester at Whitsuntide. Edited by THOMAS WRIGHT. Vol. I. 9s.

ALLEYN PAPERS; a Collection of Original Documents illustrative of the Life and Times of EDWARD ALLEYN, and of the Early English Stage and Drama. Edited by COLLIER. 4s. 6d. [A Companion to the first Article.]

"HONOUR TRIUMPHANT;" and "A LINE of LIFE." Two Tracts by JOHN FORDE, the Dramatist, recently discovered. 3s.

TARLTON'S JESTS, and NEWS OUT OF PURGATORY: with Notes, and some account of the Life of Tarlton. By J. O. HALLIWELL. 4s. 6d.

TRUE TRAGEDY of RICHARD III; to which is appended the Latin Play of RICHARDUS TERTIUS, by Dr. THOMAS LEGGE, both anterior to Shakespeare's Drama, with Notes by BARRON FIELD. 4s.

THE GHOST of RICHARD III, a Poem, 1614, founded upon Shakespeare's Historical Play, reprinted from the only known copy, edited by COLLIER. 3s. 6d.

SIR THOMAS MORE, a Play now first printed, edited by DYCE. 4s. 6d.

BY J. R. SMITH, 4, OLD COMPTON ST. SOHO. 19

THE SHAKESPEARE SOCIETY'S PAPERS, being a Miscellany of Contributions Illustrative of the Objects of the Society. Vol. I. 6s.

THE OLD TAMING OF *A* SHREW, 1594, upon which Shakespeare founded his Comedy; to which is added the WOMAN LAPPED IN MORREL SKIN. Edited by AMYOT. 4s. 6d.

N.B.—The above 31 volumes are all the Society have published.

Cambridge Antiquarian Society, 1840-44.
(*Printed in* 4to.)

CATALOGUE of the ORIGINAL LIBRARY of ST. CATHE-RINE'S HALL, 1475. Edited by PROFESSOR CORRIE. 4to, 2s. 6d.

ABBREVIATA CHRONICA, ab anno 1377, usque ad anuum 1469. Edited by the Rev. J. SMITH. 4to, *fac-simile*, 3s.

APPLICATION of HERALDRY to the Illustration of various University and Collegiate Antiquities. By H. A. WOODHAM, Esq. Part I. *coloured plate, and 30 cuts of arms*, 6s.

———————Part II, *coloured plate, and 2 woodcuts*, 3s. 6d.

ACCOUNT of the RITES and CEREMONIES which took place at the Consecration of ABP. PARKER. Edited by J. GOODWIN. 4to, *fac-simile*, 3s.

A refutation of the foolish and absurd story, commonly known as the Nag's Head Consecration.

DESCRIPTIVE CATALOGUE of the Manuscripts and Scarce Books in the Library of St. John's College, Cambridge. Part I, 4s. 6d.

——————— Part II. 4s. 6d.

ACCOUNT of the SEXTRY BARN at ELY, lately demolished. With Architectural Illustrations by PROFESSOR WILLIS. 4 *plates*, 3s.

ARCHITECTURAL NOMENCLATURE of the MIDDLE AGES. By PROFESSOR WILLIS. 3 *plates*. 7s.

REPORT of the First, Second, and Third General Meetings of the CAMBRIDGE ANTIQUARIAN SOCIETY. 8vo, 1s. each.

Publication of the Abbotsford Club.

LE ROMAN des AVENTURES de FREGUS (*an Anglo-Norman Romance.*) Par GUILLAUME LE CLERC, Trouvere du treizième siècle; publié pour la première fois par F. MICHEL. 4to, *cloth, only 60 copies printed*, 1l. 15s.

Lincolnshire Topographical Society.

A SELECTION of PAPERS relative to the COUNTY of LINCOLN, read before the Lincolnshire Topographical Society, 1841-2. Small 4to, *ten plates, cl.* 7s. 6d.

Contents: Opening address, by E. J. WILLSON, F.S.A.; Geology of Lincoln, by W. BEDFORD; The Malandry Hospital for Lepers at Lincoln, by Dr. COOKSON; Leprosy of the Middle Ages, by Dr. COOKSON; Temple Bruer and its Knights, by Dr. OLIVER; Advantage of Recording the discovery of Local Antiquities, by W. A. NICHOLSON; Tattershall Castle, by W. A. NICHOLSON.

Parker Society's Publications.—1841-44.

(*All 8vo, in cloth.*)

RIDLEY'S (BISHOP) WORKS. Edited by the Rev. H. CHRISTMAS. 10s. 6d.

SANDY'S (BISHOP) SERMONS and MISCELLANEOUS PIECES. Edited by Rev. J. AYRE. 10s. 6d.

PILKINGTON'S (BISHOP) WORKS. Edited by the Rev. J. SCHOLEFIELD. 10s. 6d.

HUTCHINSON'S (ROGER) WORKS. Edited by J. BRUCE, Esq. 10s. 6d.

PHILPOT'S (Archdeacon and Martyr, 1555) Examinations and Writings. Edited by the Rev. R. EDEN. 10s. 6d.

GRINDAL'S (ARCHBISHOP) REMAINS. Edited by the Rev. W. NICHOLSON. 10s. 6d.

ZURICH LETTERS, comprising the Correspondence of several English Bishops and others, with some of the Helvetian Reformers, temp. Q. Elizabeth, from the originals at Zurich. Edited by the Rev. H. ROBINSON. 1l. 1s.

BECON'S (Prebendary of Canterbury temp. Hen. VIII) EARLY WORKS. Edited by the Rev. J. AYRE. Royal 8vo, 10s.

CHRISTIAN PRAYERS and HOLY MEDITATIONS. Collected by H. BULL. 12mo, cloth, 6s.

FULKE'S DEFENCE of the TRANSLATIONS of the BIBLE Against GREGORY MARTIN, a CATHOLIC. Edited by HARTSHORNE. 8s. 6d.

HOOPER'S (Bishop and Martyr) EARLY WRITINGS. Edited by CARR. 8s. 6d.

BECON'S CATECHISM, and other Pieces. Edited by AYRE. Royal 8vo, 10s.

THE LUTURGIES, and other DOCUMENTS set forth by EDWARD IV. Edited by KETLEY. 8s. 6d.

COVERDALE'S (BISHOP) WRITINGS and TRANSLATIONS. Edited by PEARSON. 8s. 6d.

LATIMER'S (BISHOP) SERMONS. Edited by CORRIE. 8s. 6d.

Société Asiatique de Paris.

MENG TSEU vel MENICUM, inter Sinenses Philosophos, ingenio, doctrina nominisque claritate Confucio proximum, edidit, latina interpretum (*with the Chinese Text*) a STANISLAUS JULIEN. 2 vols. 8vo, sewed, 1l. 5s.

RODRIGUEZ, ELEMENS de la GRAMMAIRE JAPONAISE, avec Supplement par LANDRESSE et REMUSAT. 8vo, sewed, 8s.

BURNOUF et LASSEN, ESSAI sur le PALI, ou Langue Sacrée de la presqu'ile au-dela du Gange. 8vo, *six plates*, sewed, 10s.

LA RECONNAISSANCE de SACOUNTALA, Drame Sanscrit et Pracrit de CALIDASA, publié pour la première fois en original, accompagné d'une Traduction Française, de Notes philologiques, critiques et littéraires. Par A. L. CHEZY. 4to, *sewed*, 1*l*. 10*s*.

YAJNADATTABADA, ou la MORT D'YAJNADATTA, episode extrait du Ramayana, poëme épique Sanscrit, avec le texte et une traduction Française et Latine. Par CHEZY et BURNOUF. 4to, *sewed*, 12*s*.

CHRONIQUE GEORGIENNE, Traduite (avec le texte original) par M. BROSSET, jeune. 8vo, *sewed*, 7*s*.

VOCABULAIRE et GRAMMAIRE de la LANGUE GEORGIENNE. Par M. J. KLAPROTH. 8vo, *sewed*, 12*s*.

ELEGIE sur la PRISE d'EDESSE par les MUSULMANS. Par NERSES KLAIETSI, Patriarche d'Armenie; publié pour la première fois en Armenien. Par Dr. T. ZOHRAB. 8vo, *sewed*, 4*s*.

Any of the other publications of the Society will be procured by J. R. S., who has been appointed Agent to the Society in London.

MEMOIRE, LETTRES et RAPPORTS relatifs au COURS de LANGUES MALAYA et JAVANAISE, fait à la Bibliothèque Royale 1840-42, et à deux voyages littéraires entrepis en Angleterre sous les auspices de le Ministre de l'Instruction Publique, et de l'Académie Royale des Inscriptions et Belles Lettres. Par EDOUARD DULAURIER.—Paris, 1843. 8vo, *sewed, not printed for sale*, 3*s*. 6*d*.

Société de l'École Royale des Chartes.

BIBLIOTHEQUE de L'ECOLE des CHARTES, Recueil Historique, Philologique, et Littéraire. Publié par la Société de l'Ecole Royale des Chartes. Royal 8vo, handsomely printed, Vol I, (*out of print*.) Paris, 1839-40.

————————————— Vol. II, *sewed*, 12*s*. 6*d*.   1840-1.

————————————— Vol. III, *sewed*, 12*s*. 6*d*.   1841-2.

————————————— Vol. IV, *sewed*, 12*s*. 6*d*.   1842-3.

————————————— Vol. V, *sewed*, 12*s*. 6*d*.   1843-4.

Five Volumes of the Publications of this Society have appeared at 12*s*. 6*d*. per Vol., which contain many articles interesting to the English Historian and Antiquary. The succeeding volumes of the Society will be on sale by J. R. S., who has been appointed Agent to the Society for England. A Prospectus may be had on application.

BOOKS AT VERY REDUCED PRICES.

HISTORY of GERMAN LITERATURE. By WOLFGANG MENZEL. Translated from the German with Notes by THOMAS GORDON. Four Vols. post 8vo.—Oxford, 1840. *Cloth*, 15*s*., pub. at 2*l*.

A very popular work in Germany, of which there has been many editions.

HISTORY of the ORIGIN and ESTABLISHMENT of GOTHIC ARCHITECTURE, and an Inquiry into the mode of Painting upon and Staining Glass, as practised in the Ecclesiastical Structures of the Middle Ages. By JOHN SIDNEY HAWKINS, F.A.S. Royal 8vo, *eleven plates*, bds. 3*s*. 6*d*., pub. at 12*s*.

LECTURES on the COINAGE of the GREEKS and ROMANS, delivered in the University of Oxford. By EDWARD CARDWELL, D.D., Principal of St. Alban's Hall, and Professor of Ancient History. 8vo, *cl.*, REDUCED FROM 8s. 6d. to 4s.

A very interesting historical volume, and written in a pleasing and popular manner.

ARRIAN'S VOYAGE ROUND the EUXINE SEA, translated and accompanied with a Geographical Dissertation. By THOMAS FALCONER, Editor of Strabo, Hanno, &c. 4to, *with maps, and a plate of the Coins of the Cities on the Coast of the Euxine, bds.* 3s. 6d. (pub. at 1l. 15s.)

The Appendix contains—I. On the trade to the East Indies by means of the Euxine Sea. II. On the distance which the ships of antiquity usually sailed in twenty-four hours. III. On the measure of the Olympic Stadium.

ENGRAVINGS from PICTURES in the NATIONAL GALLERY, published by AUTHORITY, imp. folio, containing *twenty-nine engravings, in the line manner.* By BURNET, DOO, GOLDING, GOODALL, J. and H. LE KEUX, J. PYE, J. H. ROBINSON, &c. &c. with descriptions in English and French. *In cloth,* 10l. 10s. (pub. at 14l. 14s.)

A very choice subscriber's copy. The size of the work corresponds with the "Musée François." and the "Gallerie de Florence."

PLANS, ELEVATIONS, SECTIONS, DETAILS, and VIEWS, of the CATHEDRAL of GLASGOW. By W. COLLIE, *Architect.* Folio, 43 *fine plates, bds.* 16s. (pub. at 2l. 2s.)

The Cathedral of Glasgow is, with the solitary exception of that of Kirkwall in Orkney, the only one which escaped the destructive hands of the early Reformers, and to this day it remains one of the most entire, and at the same time the most splendid specimens of Gothic Architecture in the island.

HISTORY of the ANCIENT PALACE and late HOUSES of PARLIAMENT at WESTMINSTER, embracing Accounts and Illustrations of St. Stephen's Chapel and its Cloisters; Westminster Hall; the Court of Requests; the Painted Chamber, &c. &c. By E. W. BRAYLEY and JOHN BRITTON, Fellows of the Antiquarian Society. Thick 8vo, *illustrated with 41 fine steel engravings, by the best Artists, and 7 woodcuts chiefly from drawings by Billings,* cloth, 8s. 6d. (pub. at 21s.)

A very interesting volume to the Historian, the Antiquary, and the Architect.

NAUTICAL OBSERVATIONS on the PORT and MARITIME VICINITY of CARDIFF, with Remarks on the Taff Vale Railway, and the Commerce of Glamorganshire. By Capt. W. H. SMYTH, R.N. 8vo, *two charts, privately printed, cloth,* 2s. 6d.

DOMESDAY BOOK for the COUNTY of WARWICK, translated with the original on the opposite page. By W. READER. 4to, *only* 100 *printed, bds.* 7s. (pub. at 21s.)

A brief Dissertation on Domesday Book, compiled from various authorities, is prefixed to the translation—also, a List of the Saxon Possessors in the time of King Edward the Confessor; an Alphabetical List of the Land-owners after the Norman Invasion, with Biographical Notices; The names of the Persons who held under these Landholders; and to complete the arrangement, a copious Index of the Ancient and Modern Names of Places is added.

POPULAR ERRORS in ENGLISH GRAMMAR, particularly in Pronunciation, familiarly pointed out. By GEORGE JACKSON. 12mo, Third Edition, *with a coloured frontispiece of the "Sedes Busbiana."* 6d.

AN EXPLANATION of the ELEMENTARY CHARACTERS of the CHINESE, with an Analysis of their Ancient Symbols and Hieroglyphics. By JOSEPH HAGER, D.D. Folio, *finely printed by Bensley, a curious book, bds.* 5s.

BIBLIOTHECA SCOTO-CELTICA; or, an Account of all the Books which have been printed in the Gaelic Language, with Bibliographical and Biographical Notices. By JOHN REID. 8vo, *bds.* 5*s.* (pub. at 10*s.* 6*d.*)

PEDIGREES and ARMS of the FAMILIES in the COUNTY of SUSSEX, collected from the Heraldic Visitations, &c. By WILLIAM BERRY, fifteen years Registering Clerk in the College of Arms. Folio, *bds.* 21*s* (pub. at 6*l.* 6*s.*)

PEDIGREES and ARMS of the FAMILIES in the COUNTY of HANTS. By WILLIAM BERRY. Folio, *bds.* 1*l.* 1*s.* (pub. at 6*l.* 6*s.*)

PEDIGREES and ARMS of the FAMILIES in the COUNTIES of SURREY, BERKS, and BUCKINGHAM. By W. BERRY. Folio, *bds.* 1*l.* 18*s.* (pub. at 5*l.* 5*s.*)

PEDIGREES of the NOBILITY and GENTRY of the COUNTY of HERTS. By WILLIAM BERRY, late and for fifteeen years Registering Clerk in the College of Arms. Author of the " Encyclopædia Heraldica," &c. &c. Folio (only 150 printed), *bds,* 3*l.* 10*s.*

" These Collections of Pedigrees will be found of great utility, though not of sufficient proof in themselves to establish the claims of kindred set forth in them : but affording a ready clue to such necessary proof whenever it should be required, by pointing out the places of nativity, baptism, marriages, and burials, and such other legal documents, as localities will otherwise afford, and the modern entries in the Herald's College, are of no better authority, requiring the very same kind of proof for legal purposes. This observation will perhaps silence the ill-natured remarks which have emanated from that quarter: and it is self-evident that the printing of 250 copies is a much safer record than one manuscript entry there, which might easily be destroyed."—*Preface.*

ACCOUNT of the FOREIGN ORDERS of KNIGHTHOOD, and other marks of Honorable Distinction, especially such as have been conferred upon British Subjects. By NICHOLAS CARLISLE, *Secretary of the Antiquarian Society.* Royal 8vo, *very handsomely printed, cloth,* 8*s.* (pub. at 20*s.*)

LEGENDS of the CONQUEST of SPAIN. By WASHINGTON IRVING. Post 8vo, *bds.* 2*s.* 6*d.* (pub. at 10*s.* 6*d,*)

DOINGS in LONDON, or, DAY and NIGHT SCENES of the FRAUDS, FROLICS, MANNERS, and DEPRAVITIES of the METROPOLIS. By GEORGE SMEETON (*the curious Printer*) 8vo, 33 woodcuts by R. CRUIKSHANK, *a very amusing volume, cloth,* 4*s.* 6*d.* (pub. at 12*s.*)

HISTORY of MUHAMEDANISM, comprising the Life and Character of the Arabian Prophet, and succinct account of the Empires founded by the Muhamedan Arms. By CHARLES MILLS. 8vo, *cloth* 6*s.* (pub. at 14*s.*)

THE ORIGIN, PROGRESS, and PRESENT CONDITION of the Fine Arts in Great Britain and Ireland. By W. B. SARSFIELD TAYLOR. 2 thick vols. post 8vo, *with many woodcuts, cloth,* 8*s.* 6*d.* (pub. at 1*l.* 1*s.*)

COLECCION de OBRAS y DOCUMENTOS relativos a la HISTORIA ANTIQUA y MODERNA de las PROVINCIAS del RIO DE LA PLATA, illustrados con notas y disertaciones. Por PEDRO DE ANGELIS. 6 vols. folio, *sewed.* 6*l.* 6*s.*
Buenos Aires, 1836-7.

The most valuable and important collection of documents that has yet appeared relative to this part of the New World : they were printed at the expense of the Argentine Republic, and not for sale. Through the kindness of the editor, J. R. SMITH has been allowed to import a few copies for the purpose of being placed in some of the public libraries in England and on the Continent, or in those who take an interest in the early history and geography of the middle part of South America.

RAPPORTS à M. le MINISTRE de l'INSTRUCTION PUBLIQUE sur les ANCIENS MONUMENTS de l'Histoire et de la Littérature de la France, qui se trouvent dans les Bibliothèques de l'Angleterre et de l'Ecosse. Par FRANCISQUE MICHEL. 4to, pp. 280, *Paris, Imprimerie Royale,* 1838, *sewed,* 8*s.*

Of this interesting volume, only 200 copies were printed, at the expense of the French Government.

VALUABLE BOOKS PUBLISHED BY J. R. SMITH.

ELEMENTS of PHYSIOLOGY; being an Account of the Laws and Principles of the Animal Economy, especially in reference to the Constitution of Man. By T. J. AITKIN, M.D. Thick post 8vo, woodcuts, cloth, 3s., published at 9s.

A MANUAL of the HISTORY of the MIDDLE AGES, from the Invasion of the Barbarians to the Fall of Constantinople; with Genealogical Tables of the Imperial Houses of Germany, of the three French Dynasties, and of the Norman-Augevin Kings of England, translated from the French Work of DES MICHELS, by T. G. JONES. 12mo, cloth, 2s. 6d., published at 6s. 6d.

" The general scarcity of elementary works on History, and more especially of such as refer to the Middle Ages, might, in itself, be a sufficient apology for the appearance of the following translation; but when it is further considered that the original text has passed through several editions, and that its reputation is established in a country confessedly eminent in historical literature, it is believed that the work, in its present form, cannot but prove a desideratum to the English student."

A ROT AMONG THE BISHOPS, or a Terrible Tempest in the Sea of Canterbury, set forth in lively Emblems to please the judicious Reader, in Verse. By THOMAS STIRRY, 1641. 18mo, (a satire on Abp. Laud,) four very curious woodcut emblems, cloth, 3s.

A facsimile of the very rare original edition which sold at Bindley's sale for 13l.

MIRROUR of JUSTICES, written originally in the old French, long before the Conquest, and many things added by Andrew Horne, translated by W. HUGHES, of Gray's Inn. 12mo, cloth, 2s.

A curious, interesting, and authentic treatise on ancient English Law.

FRENCH COOKERY adapted to English Tastes and English Pockets, with the Cost of each Dish. By R. MACDONALD, English-French Cook. 12mo, 1s.

BOOKS IN THE PRESS.

COMPENDIOUS ANGLO-SAXON and ENGLISH DICTIONARY. By the Rev. JOSEPH BOSWORTH, D.D., F.R.S., F.S.A., &c.

It will contain all the words of the large octavo edition, with numerous additions, and will be published at a price which will place it within the reach of of all who take an interest in the language of their forefathers.

GUIDE to the ANGLO-SAXON TONGUE; for the use of beginners, on the basis of Professor Rask's Grammar. By E. J. VERNON, B.A., Oxon. Post 8vo.

BIBLIOTHECA MADRIGALIANA. A Catalogue of Musical and Poetical works published in England under the title of "Madrigals," "Ayres," &c., during the reigns of Elizabeth and James I. By EDWARD F. RIMBAULT, Ph. D. F.S.A., Member of the Royal Academy of Music in Stockholm, Hon. Sec. to the Musical Antiquarian Society. In 8vo, price 5s.

SPECULATIONS on the HISTORY of PLAYING-CARDS in EUROPE. By W. A. CHATTO. 8vo, with numerous Engravings.

J. R. S. begs to call the attention of Book-buyers to his "OLD BOOK CATALOGUE," which is published every few weeks, offering a constant variety of Valuable and Cheap Books. POSTAGE FREE to those gentlemen who will favour the Publisher with their Addresses.

J. R. S. will be happy to publish on Commission, any Historical, Antiquarian, or Topographical work, and will give it every publicity through the medium of his Catalogues, &c. without cost to the Proprietor.

PRINTED BY C. AND J. ADLARD, BARTHOLOMEW CLOSE.